Our Father's World

2

Rod and Staff Publishers, Inc.
P.O. Box 3, Hwy. 172
Crockett, Kentucky 41413
Telephone: 606-522-4348

Acknowledgments

"Thus saith the LORD, . . . I have made the earth, and created man upon it. . . . God . . . hath established [the earth], he created it not in vain, he formed it to be inhabited: I am the LORD; and there is none else" (Isaiah 45:11–18).

Writer: Brenda McDowell

Editor: Robert McDowell

Artists: Susie Hoover; Lester Miller

Printed in U.S.A.

ISBN 978-07399-0638-5

Catalog no. 19221

20 21 22 23 — 21 20 19 18 17 16 15 14

Contents

4. A Day in the Continents

5. Reading Maps

1. Different Kinds of Lands

All nature sings, and round me rings
The music of the spheres.

1. Hill Country

Dorcas and John Byer sat quietly in the car watching the light of the morning sun rise in the eastern sky. The Byer family had risen early and started off from their home in Eastern **Ontario** (onˈtâr•ē•ō) to visit an uncle in British Columbia. As they traveled north, white light began to color the sky between the hilltops to their right. Slowly the sky changed to a light pink, and then to a brighter pink, as the sun rose toward the horizon.

"God made the sunrise beautiful," John exclaimed.

"And the hills and the many kinds of trees too," added Mother. "The hillside looks like a carpet. Look at all the different shades of green. The evergreens are dark green, the poplars are light green, and the maples are the color of grass. It makes a pretty picture."

"The trees are sawn into **lumber** (ˈlum•bər) at a sawmill to make homes, chairs, tables, beds, and other things, aren't they?" asked Dorcas.

"They are a shelter for deer, wolves, bear, foxes, raccoons, and other animals too," Father told them.

A fawn (young deer) hiding under a tree canopy.

Soon they saw a few houses along the side of the road. "The people in this **village** (ˈvil•ij) must be asleep yet," said Father. "This little **country** (ˈkun•trē) store will probably not open until 8 o'clock."

"We won't be able to get gas there," John thought.

After passing the village, they came to a hay field that reached to the edge of the road. Large rocks were sticking out of the ground. Near the road on a rock sat a groundhog. Close by was a hole that led to his home in the ground.

A groundhog sitting on a rock.

Up and down hills and around corners the road led the Byer family. Here and there beside the road they saw a house and sometimes a little barn or shed nearby.

"Father, why is the water so close to the road?" John asked as he stared at the water. Much water lay beside a flat stretch of road between the hills. "The water is even among the trees!"

"The beavers must have been busy here," Father explained. "Somewhere in this woods you could find a beaver **dam** (dam), and a beaver house, and maybe more than one house. Men need to blast the dams to get rid of the water so it will not kill the trees."

"Does the water ever cover the roads?" Dorcas asked.

"Sometimes that happens," Father explained. "The beavers have built large dams that cover one or two hectares (two and one-half to five acres) of fields and woodland. Trees die if they stand in the water very long."

A beaver dam that has been blasted.

CROSSWORD PUZZLE

Read the description below. Find where the word should be written in the puzzle. Fill in the puzzle with the correct word from the story.

Across

4. A few houses near each other is called a ___.
5. A beaver dam stops the flow of ___.
7. Village people buy groceries and hardware at a ___ ___.
9. Beavers build ___ to hold back the water.
10. A ___ lives in a hole in the ground.
11. A ___ is a large black animal that lives in the woods.
12. ___ are red or grey animals as large as a medium-size dog.

Down

1. ___ are as tall as a large dog, and they howl.
2. A farmer keeps his cattle in a ___.
3. ___ are night animals that live in holes in trees.
6. Tall, green ___ grow on the hills.
8. Beavers build ___ to live in.
9. A ___ is a reddish brown animal as tall as a large calf, and can run swiftly through the woods.

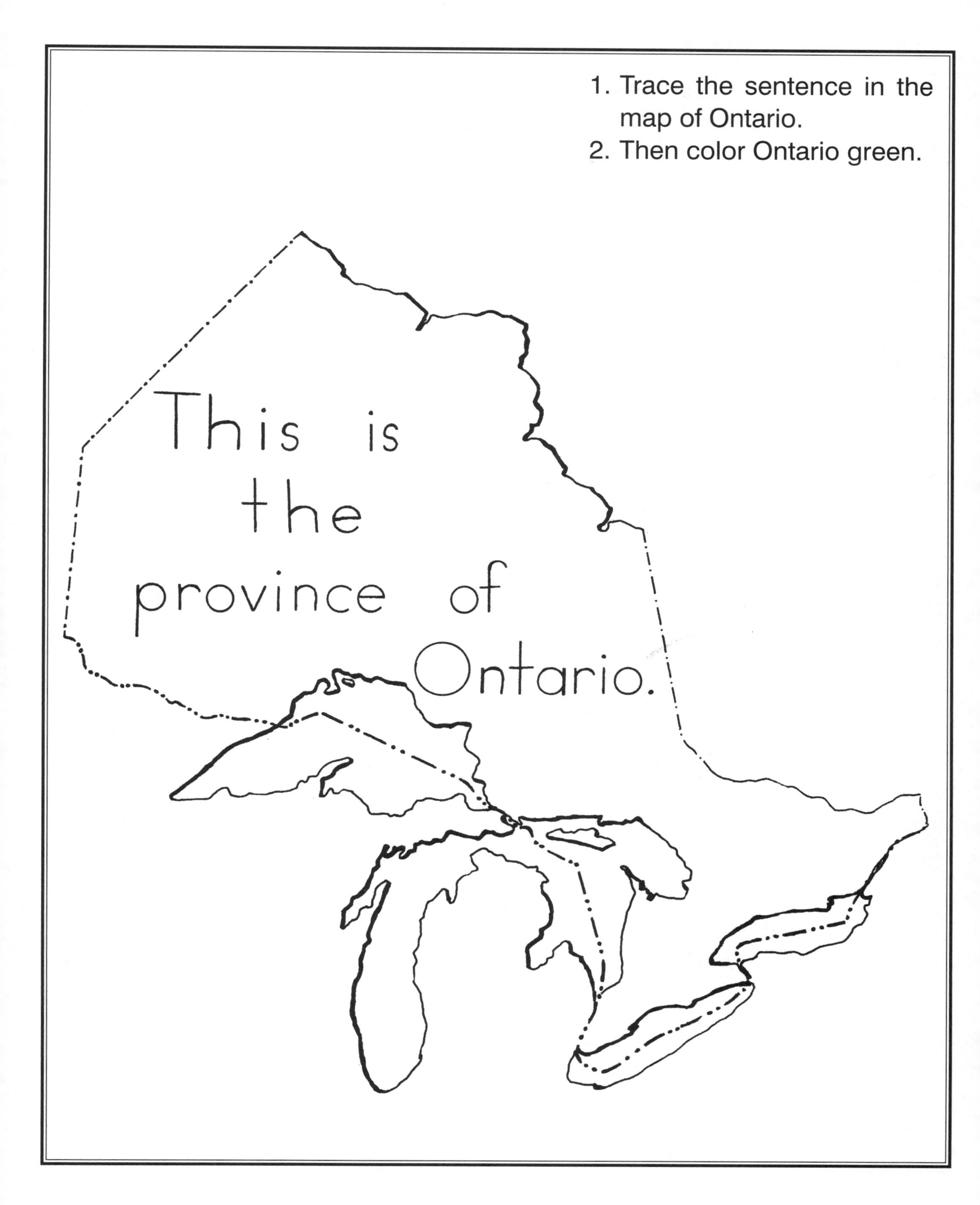
1. Trace the sentence in the map of Ontario.
2. Then color Ontario green.
This is the province of Ontario.

A
B
C

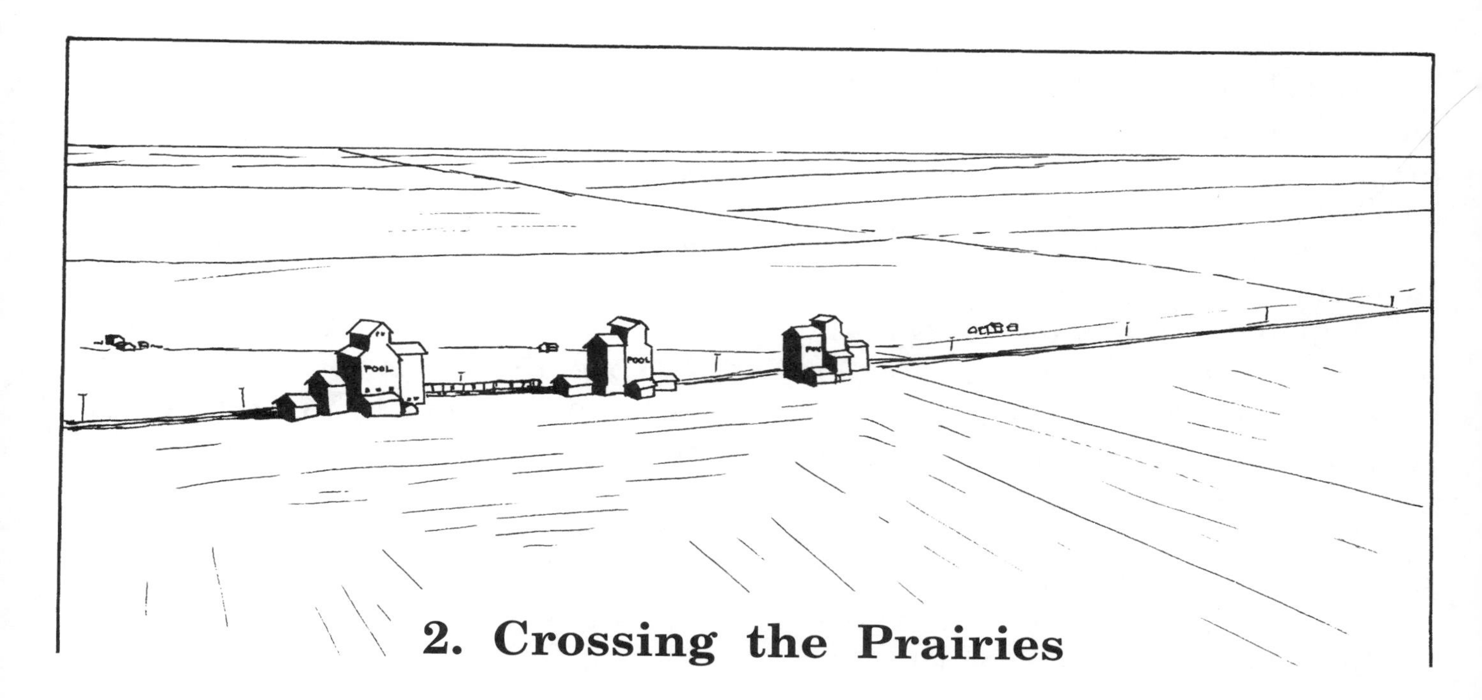

2. Crossing the Prairies

For two days the Byer family drove in Ontario. They were traveling west. In the morning the sun shone in the back window. In the afternoon the sun shone in the front window.

"See the sign?" Father asked soon after they began their third day of travel. "It reads, 'Welcome to **Manitoba** (ˈman•eˈtō•bə).' Manitoba is the next **province** (ˈprov•ins) of Canada west of Ontario. Soon the land will be flatter. We are leaving the hill country and will be in the **prairie** (ˈprâr•ē). Manitoba is one of the three Prairie Provinces."

"Will we be in British Columbia today?" Dorcas asked.

"No, not today," Father replied.

Soon they reached the open prairie and passed by field after field of crops.

A ship hauling grain to other countries.

"What is planted here?" John wanted to know. "The fields are really green."

"Large fields of wheat and barley are raised here on the prairie," Father told them. "It won't be long until they are golden and ready to harvest. The grain will be stored in buildings called grain **elevators** (ˈel•əˈvā•tərz). Later some of it will be loaded on ships to be sold to other countries."

"Is that a dog ahead of us on the side of the road?" Dorcas asked.

"We'll have to see," answered Father. "We'll drive slower when we pass it so we can find out."

Just before they reached the doglike animal, it trotted off the road and then broke into a run.

"It wasn't the color of a fox, and I don't think it was a wolf," John guessed thoughtfully.

"No, it wasn't a wolf or a fox. It was a **coyote** (kī ˈō•tē)," Mother told them.

Later in the day, as they reached the rolling plain in western Manitoba, John's attention was attracted by a large herd of cattle feeding in a grass field. "They aren't black and white like most cows I've seen," he pointed out. "They are reddish brown."

Beef cattle grazing in a field.

"These cattle are beef cattle," Father explained. "They are sold for meat when they are fully grown."

Soon after they entered the second Prairie Province, **Saskatchewan** (sasˈkach•ə•won), Mother sighted some grain elevators far ahead. "Let's guess how many kilometers we will have to drive until we are beside them," Mother suggested.

"I'll say 3 kilometers (about two miles)," said Dorcas.

"I'll say 5 kilometers (over three miles)," John decided.

"My guess is 20 (about twelve and one-half miles)," estimated Father.

"I'll say 15 (over nine miles)," Mother finally determined.

"Three kilometers (about two miles) are up, and we're not there yet," Father announced a little later.

"I didn't think it would take this long!" Dorcas exclaimed. "They are still a great way off."

After driving for ten more minutes, they were nearing the elevators, which now looked much larger than at first.

"You win, Father," Mother told him. "It is 18 kilometers (over eleven miles), and you said 20, so you are closest."

"Eighteen kilometers! That's a long way," said Dorcas. "We can't see that far down our winding roads at home."

On the fourth day they entered the third Prairie Province, **Alberta** (al'bûr•tə). Here the children saw a strange sight.

"How did those big piles of sand get there?" asked John.

"What you see are **sand dunes** ('sand do͞onz)," explained Father. "Wind storms carry the sand here from fields where nothing is growing."

"It looks like a big field of sand," said Dorcas.

"Yes, it does," agreed Father.

Sand piled up by the wind.

CAN YOU FIND THE ANSWERS?

Choose one of the words below to fill in the blanks.

1. The Byer family lives in the province of ______________.
2. In our story today, they entered the provinces of ______________, ______________, and ______________.
3. The ______________ is an animal that lives on the prairies and looks nearly like a dog.
4. ______________ cattle feed on the grassland in the Prairie Provinces.
5. Name two crops that grow in the prairies. ______________ ______________
6. The fields turn ______________ (a color) before they are harvested.
7. ______________ is stored in large buildings called elevators.
8. ______________ carry the grain to other countries.
9. The Byer family saw ______________ ______________ that had been heaped up by the wind.

wheat	coyote	golden	Saskatchewan	sand dunes	Manitoba
beef	Alberta	Grain	Ontario	barley	Ships

THE PRAIRIE PROVINCES

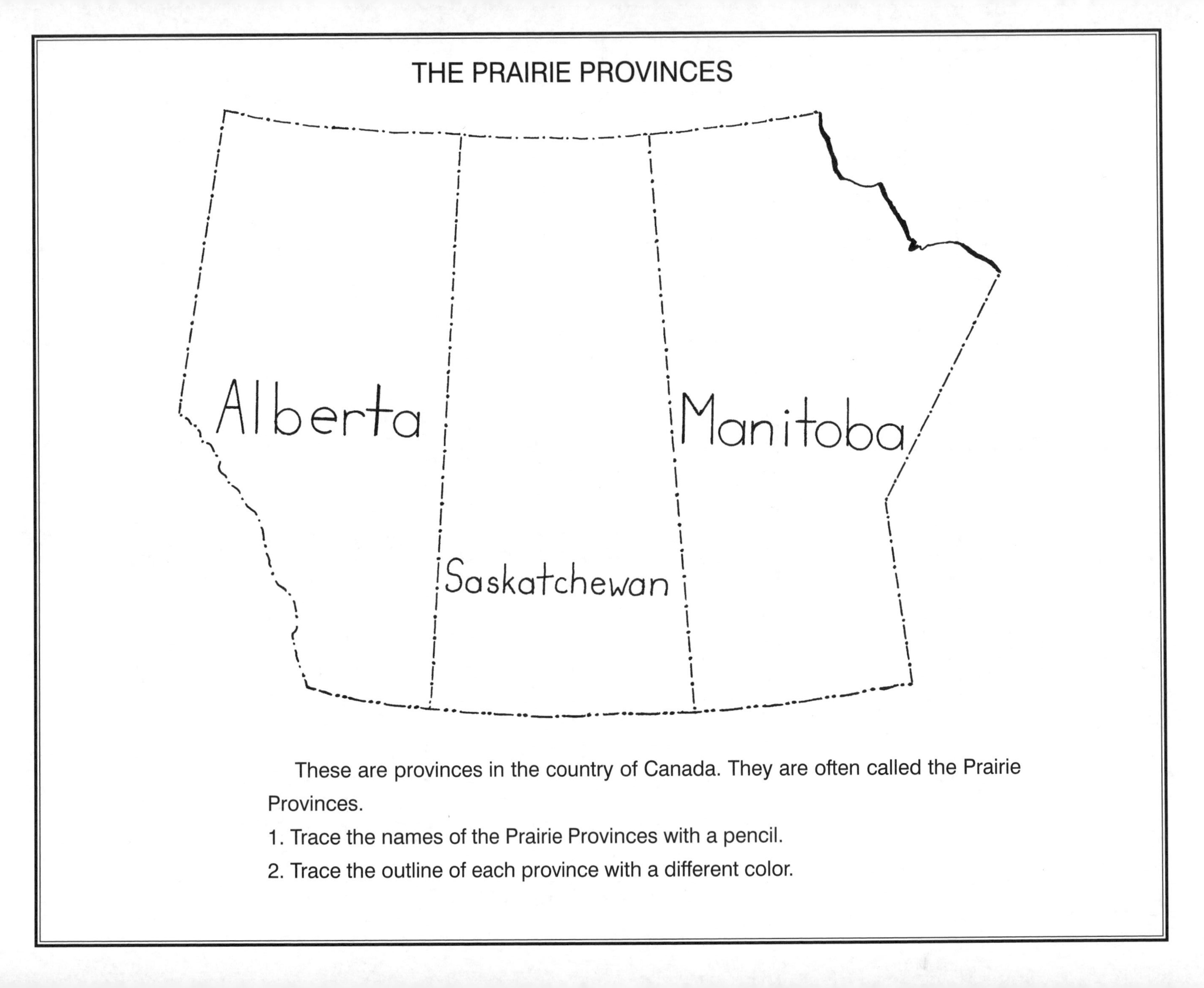

These are provinces in the country of Canada. They are often called the Prairie Provinces.

1. Trace the names of the Prairie Provinces with a pencil.
2. Trace the outline of each province with a different color.

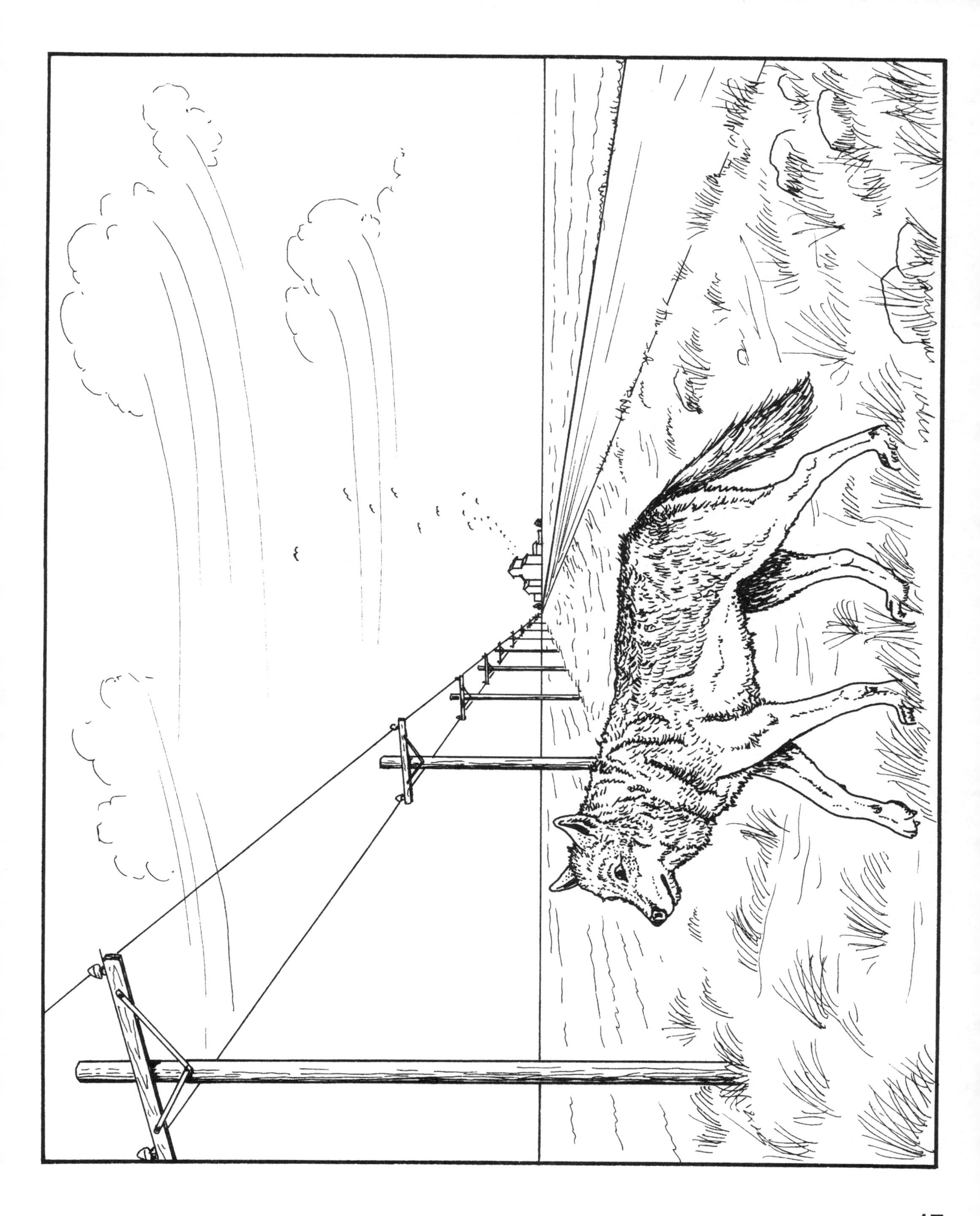

3. Sighting the Mountains

"See the **foothills** (ˈfo͝ot ˈhilz) of the **Rocky Mountains** (ˈrok•ē ˈmoun•tənz) up ahead!" Father explained in the morning on the fifth day of their trip.

John and Dorcas quickly leaned over the front seat, gazing in the direction Father had been looking.

"Foothills, what are they?" John wanted to know.

"Lower hills at the bottom of mountains," Father told him. "Right now clouds are covering the Rockies and the tops of the foothills, but soon the clouds will disappear, and then you will be able to see the tops of the foothills."

"Dorcas, look at all the hills out there," said John looking out his window.

"There are many hills out here too," said Dorcas, looking out her window. "They reach as far as I can see!"

"The mountains and their foothills are a part of a large **mountain range** (rānj) that stretches across the length of our land," Father informed them.

The clouds gradually disappeared just as Father had said. The closer they got to the hills, the higher up they could see. Trees seemed to cover the hills like a blotched green carpet.

"Are the Rocky Mountains in British Columbia?" John asked.

"They are partly in British Columbia and partly in Alberta," Father replied.

"Will we be in British Columbia today?" Dorcas wondered.

"Yes," answered Father. "We will be in British Columbia today, the Lord willing."

"Look at that steep **slope** (slōp),"

A steep mountain slope.

Mother pointed out.

"I wouldn't want to toboggan down there," Dorcas remarked. "I guess there is no snow on the hills to toboggan on now anyway, but that hill looks too steep."

"Soon you will be able to see snow," Father told them.

"Snow!" John exclaimed in surprise. "Snow in the summertime?"

"When we get high enough in the foothills to see the mountains, then you will see snow," Father explained.

"Oh-h-h!" said John as the mountains came in view. "I never saw such high mountains."

The timber line and snowline on a mountain.

"Are they ever high!" Dorcas exclaimed. "Why are they so white at the top?"

"The higher up the mountains we go, the colder it becomes," Father informed them. "At the peaks of many mountains, the temperature never becomes warm enough to melt all the ice and snow. Therefore, the tops of many mountains are always covered with a cap of ice and snow. Do you see the rocks and grass below the **snow line** (ˈsnō līn)?"

"It's hard to tell what it is because it's so far away," Mother said.

"All I can see are the trees, but they don't reach as high as the snow line," remarked John. "It seems as if they only go so far up the mountain and then they stop."

"That's the edge of the **timberline** (ˈtim•bər līn)," Father explained. "Only grass and shrubs will grow above the timberline because it is so cold."

"Father, the trees are bigger near the bottom of the mountain, aren't they?" Mother questioned.

"Yes, they usually are," Father agreed.

"How big are they?" Dorcas wanted to know.

"Douglas firs grow to be as wide as you can reach when you stretch out both arms," Father began. "Farther west are the Coastal Ranges, which also stretch down into the United States. In the **state** (stāt) of **California** (ˈkal• ə ˈfôrn•yə) are trees called **redwoods** (ˈred•wo͝odz). Men cut a tunnel through one of them that is large enough to drive a car through."

"A car!" John and Dorcas exclaimed, looking at each other in surprise.

"I'd like to see a picture of that sometime," John said hopefully.

"Maybe you can at Uncle Samuel's," Mother said with a smile.

CAN YOU FIND THE ANSWERS?

Write the letter of the word or words at the right beside the matching meaning.

_____ 1. Upward or downward slant, as a hillside.	a. timberline
_____ 2. A hilly region at the bottom of a mountain range.	b. mountain range
_____ 3. The line above which no trees grow on a mountain.	c. foothills
_____ 4. The name for a large tree in California.	d. snow line
_____ 5. The area above which there is snow all summer.	e. redwood
_____ 6. A long line of mountains.	f. slope

Think carefully as you answer these questions.

7. Number the terms below from 1–6 to tell what you would see as you look from the top of the mountain to the bottom of the mountain.

_____ grass and shrubs

_____ valley

_____ snow line

_____ timberline

_____ a cap of snow

_____ large trees

8. Why are there no trees growing above the timberline? ____________________

____

9. Why does the snow at the mountain peak not melt away in the summer time?

____

4. Viewing the Valley

"Down the mountainside we go!" Father said as they followed the winding road. "Some of these roads are quite narrow. There isn't much room to pass another car."

"I wouldn't want to get off the edge on this side of the road," Mother commented, looking out her window. "The mountain is so steep and rocky that people would be killed if their car went over the edge."

"Has anyone ever gone over the edge of a **cliff** (klif) like this?" John wondered.

"Yes, sometimes we hear of it happening," Father explained. Pointing down toward the valley, he added. "There goes a train along the **valley floor** (ˈval•ē flôr)."

"It doesn't look very big from up here," Dorcas said, "Does the train track stay close to the river all the time?"

A car on a mountain ledge.

A train traveling along the valley floor.

"No, it doesn't," Mother told her. "Sometimes the track follows a **ledge** (lej) along the mountainside, or the

A train on a mountain ledge.

train may follow a long tunnel through the mountain."

"Look," John pointed out. "There is green grass in the valley, and it looks as though there are some buildings there too. Are these farms in the valleys?"

A village in the valley.

"Very little land is level enough to farm. We will see a sawmill, however, before we get to Uncle Samuel's," Father told them. "Here in **British Columbia** (ˈbrit•ish kə ˈlum•bē•ə) there are many trees, so logging is very important."

A truck loaded with logs.

"See the waterfalls!" Mother exclaimed.

"I do," John and Dorcas declared together.

"And look at the snow and ice on the mountain over there. That's a **glacier** (ˈglā•shər), isn't it, Mother?" asked John.

"Yes," Mother replied. "Snow and ice reach like a frozen river down the mountainside. During the winter the snow piles up. Then in the spring the drifts melt and settle. When they freeze, another layer of ice is formed on the mountainside."

Glacier

"Why are those wires going up that mountain side?" asked John.

"Those are cables, and that is a **chair lift** (ˈchâr lift)," Father told him. "One time Grandfather and Grandmother sat on a chair hanging from cables and had a ride up the mountainside."

"What did they see?" John wondered.

"Grandfather and Grandmother could look far around and see the pretty mountains and valleys," Mother explained. "They said they saw a mountain goat below them when they were part way up."

"After we go through that narrow passage between two mountain peaks ahead, we will be almost at Uncle Samuel's," Father told them. "A narrow passage between two mountain peaks is called a **mountain pass** (pas)," he explained.

"Then we will soon see Jonathan and Mary," John rejoiced. "I can hardly wait to see them."

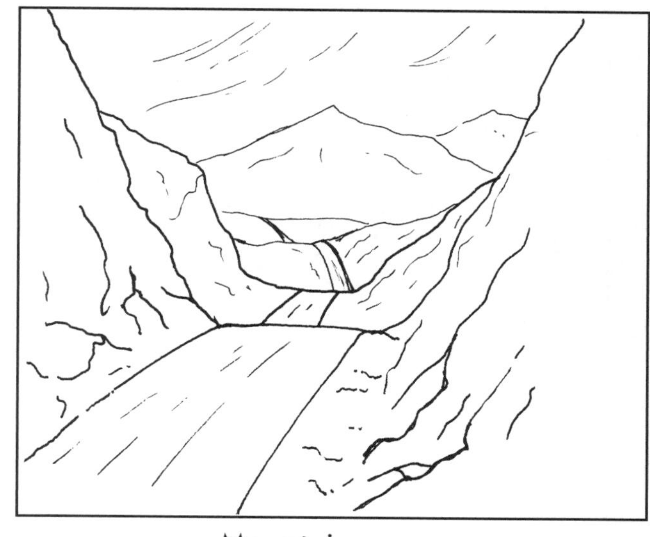

Mountain pass

LEARNING THE CORRECT NAMES

1. On the mountain scene on the next page, you will find six blanks. In the box in the upper right corner, are six names. Place these names on the correct line.
2. Color the picture.

train
mountain pass
mountain goat
glacier
valley
river
1
2
3
4
5
6

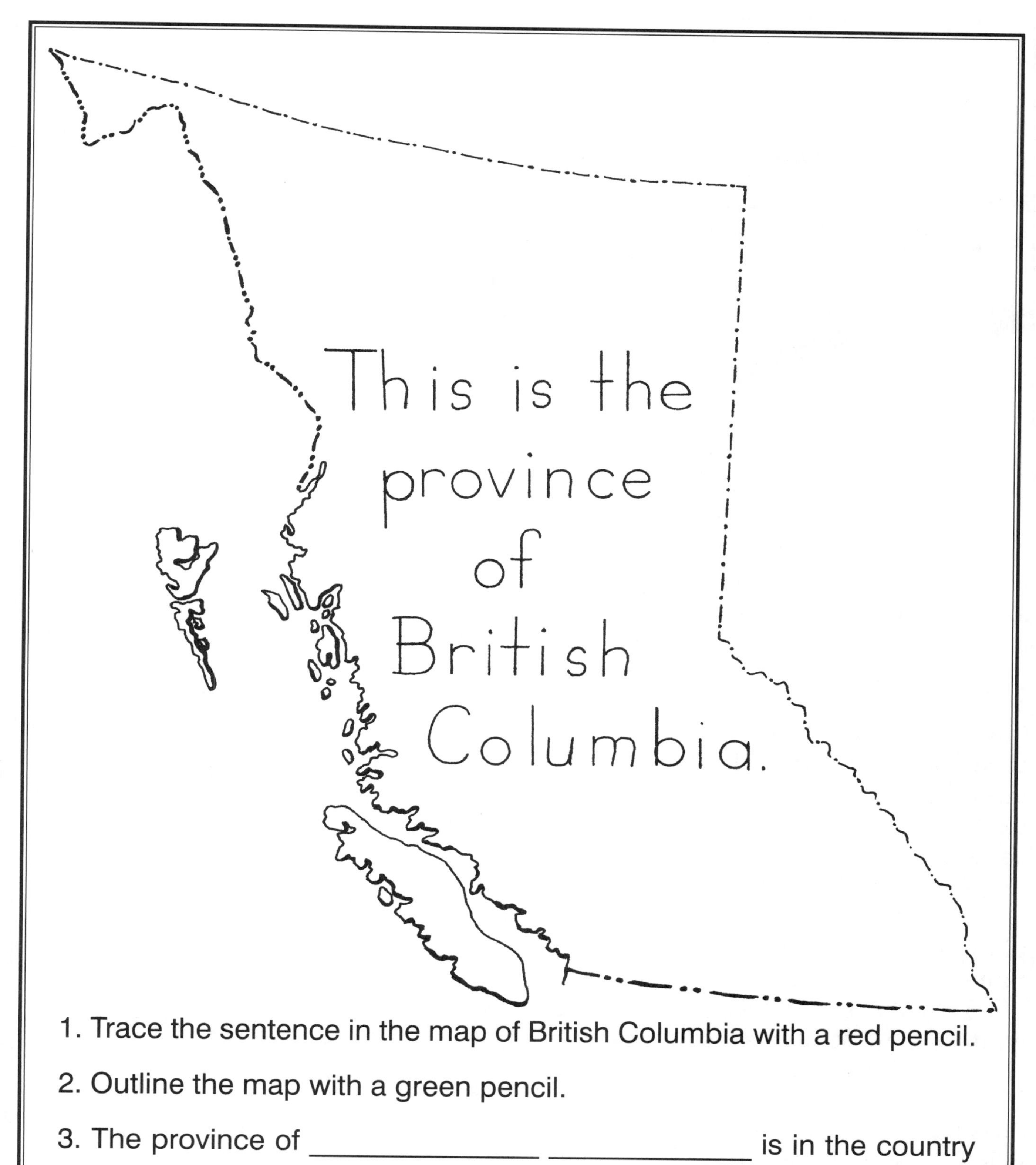

1. Trace the sentence in the map of British Columbia with a red pencil.
2. Outline the map with a green pencil.
3. The province of ______________ ______________ is in the country of ______________.

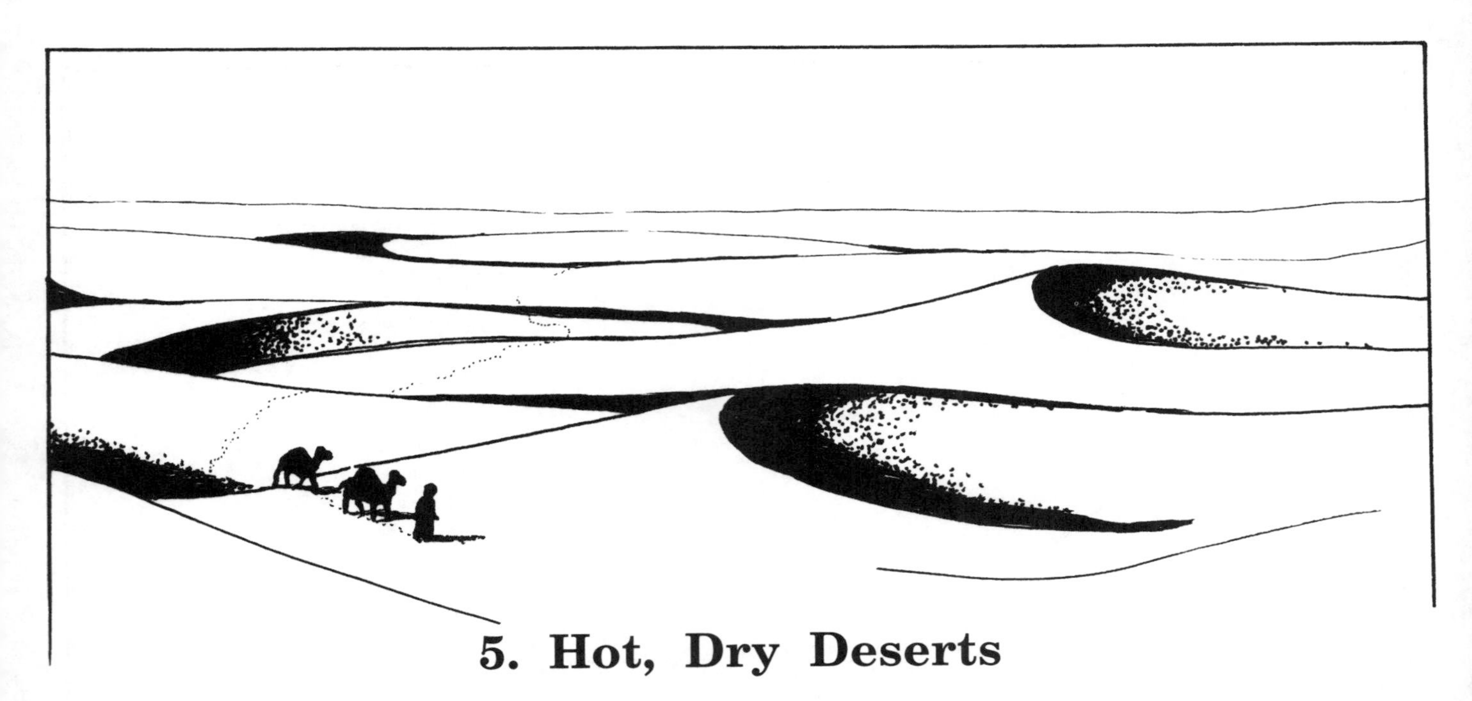

5. Hot, Dry Deserts

"This looks interesting!" exclaimed Aunt Sarah as she entered the living room. Uncle Samuel was sitting in his armchair while Jonathan, John, Dorcas, and Mary were sitting on the sofa.

"Last night Uncle Samuel told us of an unusual happening. A **desert** (ˈdez•ərt) land had snow for the first time that people can remember. It is the largest desert in the world. He's telling us more now," John told Aunt Sarah as she sat down near Uncle Samuel.

"A desert is a region that receives so very little rain that almost no plant or animal can live there," Uncle Samuel continued.

"Why don't they have snow in the wintertime?" Mary wanted to know.

"Most deserts are near the **equator** (iˈkwā•tər). At the equator the sun is directly overhead much of the year, so it is very hot. In addition, hot winds blow across the land. The winds take the water from the ground," Uncle Samuel answered. "Do you know who once lived near this desert?"

"No," the listeners said, shaking their heads.

"Moses, Aaron, and Miriam lived in the land of **Egypt** (ˈē•jipt) not far from this desert," Uncle Samuel told them.

"What is its name?" John asked.

"It is very similar to your Aunt Sarah's name," Uncle Samuel answered. "It is called the **Sahara** (səˈhar•ə) **Desert**."

Palm trees and grass near a desert spring.

"The people who live there would not need a fire to keep them warm in the winter, would they?" Dorcas asked.

"No, that's true," Uncle Samuel told her, "though very few people can live there because it is too hot. People need food, but not many plants grow in the desert."

"Aren't there any trees or grass?" John asked in surprise.

"Sometimes there is an **oasis**

A family camping in a desert.

(ō ˈā•sis) in the desert, where gardens can be planted. The gardens receive moisture from a spring. Palm trees and grass grow near the spring too," Uncle Samuel explained.

"Do deer and bear live near the spring too?" asked Dorcas.

"Not deer or bear," Uncle Samuel told them with a smile. "But the **camel** (ˈkam•əl) is a desert animal. It can walk a long time on the sandy desert

Camel

without drinking water. It stores its food in its hump. When it gets to a spring, it drinks water and eats the food it needs."

"Some people do live in the desert, but they need to move often," Aunt Sarah added. "Their animals soon eat up the grass in one spot, so the people move on to a new oasis where there is more grass."

DRAWING A PICTURE

Above is a picture of a family camping at an oasis in the desert. See the palm trees, tent, camel, green plants, and grass. **Draw a picture like this one.**

6. Review

Beside each number write one of the letters below (*a, b, c, d,* or *e*) to tell in which type of land the following are found or were seen by the children in our story.

____ 1. high peaks

____ 2. dry, sandy

____ 3. groundhog

____ 4. mountain goats

____ 5. coyote

____ 6. glaciers

____ 7. winding river

____ 8. beaver dam

____ 9. a spring with palm trees near

____ 10. grain elevators

____ 11. wheat

____ 12. beaver house

____ 13. mountain range

____ 14. foothills

____ 15. sand dunes

____ 16. snow line

____ 17. mountain pass

____ 18. very little rain

____ 19. camels

____ 20. chairlift

a. hill country b. prairie c. mountains d. valley e. desert

On the line after each number below and on the next page, write the type of land from *a, b, c, d,* or *e* above to describe the area that is shown in each picture.

21. ______________________________

22. ______________________________

23. ______________________________

24. 

25. ______________________________

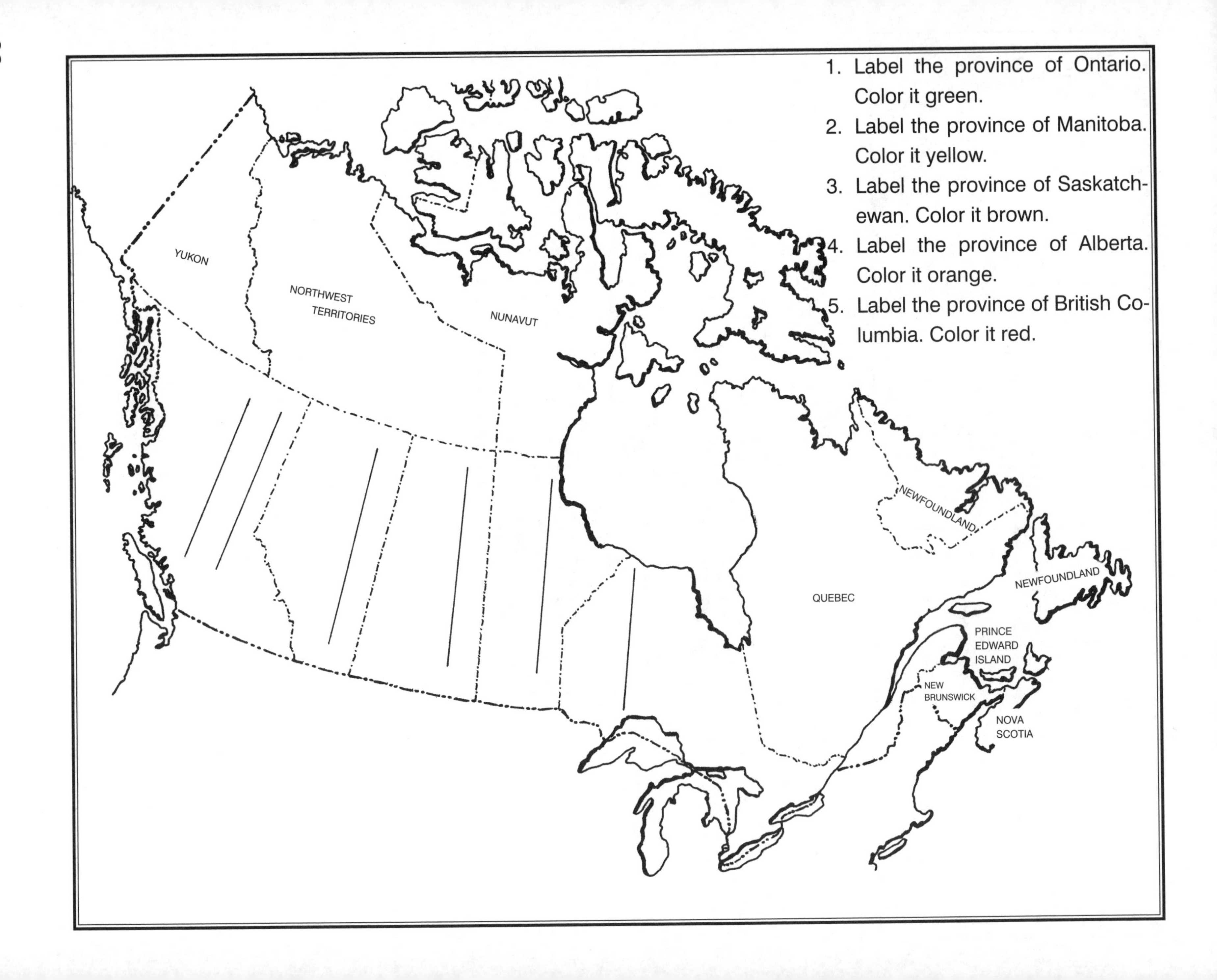

1. Label the province of Ontario. Color it green.
2. Label the province of Manitoba. Color it yellow.
3. Label the province of Saskatchewan. Color it brown.
4. Label the province of Alberta. Color it orange.
5. Label the province of British Columbia. Color it red.

2. Introducing Maps

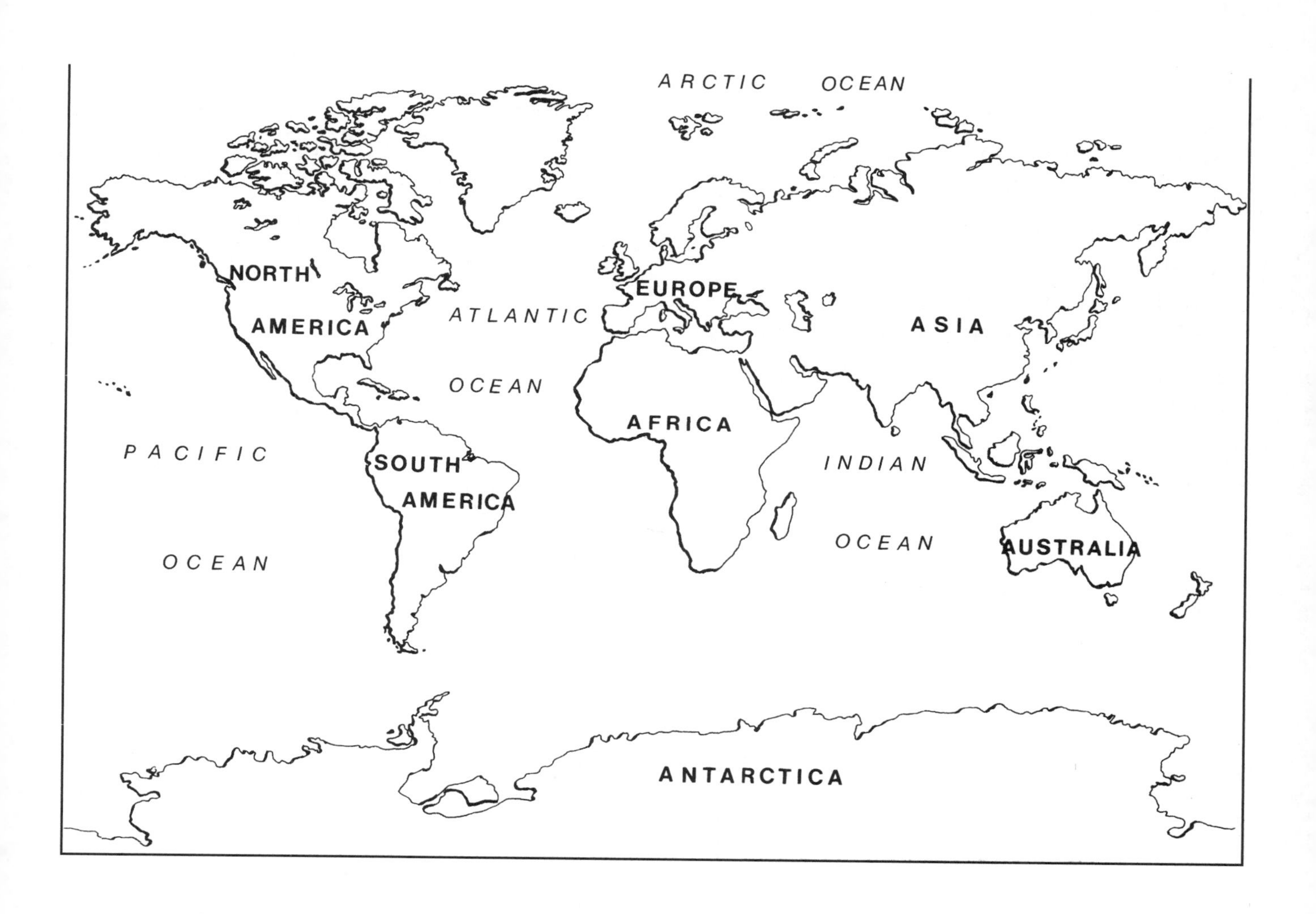

That though the wrong seems oft so strong,
God is the Ruler yet.

7. North America and South America

"On Thursday our teacher showed us on a map in which part of Canada we live," Jonathan said looking at John.

"I don't understand maps very well," John told him.

"I will get an **atlas** (ˈat•ləs) and show you where you live," Uncle Samuel said, getting up to get the atlas from the bookshelf. "I'll put it on the table where everyone can see."

Mary and Dorcas approached the table and eagerly watched as Uncle Samuel turned the pages.

"Here is a map of **North America** (əˈmer•ə•kə)," Uncle Samuel told them. "North America is the **continent** (ˈkon•tə•nənt) in which we live."

"Where do we live?" John questioned excitedly.

"Give Uncle Samuel a chance, and he will show you," Father said with a smile. "Geography is interesting."

"North America is divided into several areas called countries. The country near the top of the map is **Canada** (ˈkan•ə•də)," Uncle Samuel explained. "It is the largest country in North America. The southern part of Canada is divided into provinces. Ontario is a province of Canada.

Uncle Samuel pointing to Ontario on a map of Canada.

"The country below Canada on the map is the **United States** (yo͞oˈnī•tid ˈstātz)," he continued. "It is the second largest country in North America. Many more people live in the United States than in Canada, however. The

United States is divided into regions called *states.*

"The third largest country in North America is **Mexico** (ˈmek•sə•kō). It is below the United States. You can see that it is smaller than either Canada or the United States. Mexico is also divided into smaller regions called states.

"This part of Canada is where we are now," said Uncle Samuel, pointing to British Columbia in the far west (the part of Canada at the far left). "This is where you live," he added, moving his finger east to Ontario and looking at John and Dorcas.

"Do you know what the blue on the map is?" Father asked.

"Sister Miriam told us about blue on maps," Jonathan answered. "It is water."

"Notice that almost all of North America is surrounded by water," Father pointed out.

"What is below Mexico?" John wanted to know.

"Several small countries. They are a part of North America but are called Central America," Uncle Samuel told him. "We cannot see all of them on this map."

Carefully Uncle Samuel turned the pages in the atlas until he found the map he wanted. "This shows Central America, which is this narrow neck of land divided into seven countries."

"I see blue for water on both sides of the land," Dorcas said.

"Are there countries below Central America?" Jonathan wondered.

"There is another continent below Central America," Father explained. "It is called **South America.** It looks like an upside-down pear. Let's count the countries of South America."

"One, two, . . ." the children counted as Father pointed, "twelve, thirteen."

"Thirteen countries!" Mary exclaimed. "South America has more countries than North America."

"The countries in South America don't look as large as Canada or the United States though," John observed.

"No, they aren't," Uncle Samuel agreed. He pointed to the map. "The three largest countries in South America are **Brazil** (brəˈzil), **Argentina** (ˈär•jənˈtē•nə), and **Peru** (pəˈro͞o)."

"Now I know the names of two continents, North America and South America," Jonathan said happily. "I want to tell Sister Miriam when I get back to school."

"Maybe we will tell you about the other five continents another time," Father said. "But I think this is enough for tonight."

"Two plus five makes seven, so that means there are seven continents," John concluded.

PLACING COUNTRIES ON A MAP

Follow the directions carefully.

1. On page 35 is a map of North America. On page 131, you will find the North America cutouts for this lesson. Cut out the countries, and then paste each on the map in the correct place.

2. The three largest countries in North America are Canada, the United States, and Mexico. Write each name on the line in the correct country.

3. On page 36 is a map of South America. On page 133 you will find the South America cutouts for this lesson. Cut out the countries and paste them on the map in the correct place.

4. The three largest countries in South America are Brazil, Argentina, and Peru. Write each name on the line in the correct country.

NORTH AMERICA

SOUTH AMERICA

8. Five More Continents

"Mother," John said as he entered the kitchen where Mother was helping Aunt Sarah. "We want to have a geography match, but we have no one to name the places for us. Will you do that, please?"

"Maybe I can for a little while," Mother said, "but I would like to help Aunt Sarah again soon."

"Jonathan and Dorcas are on one team, and John and I are on the other," Mary told Mother.

"All right," said Mother. "I will name a place, and Jonathan and John will try to find it. Mary and Dorcas will try to find the next place I name. The first place I'll name is Asia (ˈā•zhə)," Mother began. "It is the largest continent. The name is

on the map in capital letters. It is spelled A-S-I-A."

After an eager search between Jonathan and John, Jonathan declared excitedly. "I have it."

"You're right," said Mother. "That is one point for Jonathan and Dorcas. This time I'll give you the second largest continent to look for. Dorcas and Mary, see if you can find **Africa** (ˈaf•ri•kə). The longest river in the world is found on this continent."

Hurrying to the map, the two girls began their search.

"It is close to the center of the map," Mother hinted. "It is spelled A-F-R-I-C-A."

"Here it is," Dorcas said.

"The next is the third largest continent. It is North America," Mother told them.

"That's easy," said John as he pointed quickly to the correct spot on the map. "Father and Uncle Samuel told us about it last night."

"The fourth largest continent is South America," Mother told them.

Dorcas and Mary raced to the map, each wondering if the other remembered that Uncle Samuel and Father had shown it to them in the atlas. "I have it," they sang out together.

"I think you both get a point," Mother said with a smile. "That was

a tie."

"The fifth largest continent is **Antarctica** (antˈärk•tə•kə)," Mother continued. "It might be harder to find."

The boys searched hard but could not find it.

"Look at the bottom of the map," Mother hinted. "It is spelled A-N-T-A-R-C-T-I-C-A."

"A-N-T-" John began spelling. "Here it is!"

"Only two more continents, and then I want to help in the kitchen," Mother told them. "The sixth largest continent is Europe (ˈyo͝or•əp)."

"How is it spelled?" Dorcas wanted to know.

"E-U-R-O-P-E," answered Mother.

"We looked on the lefthand side of the map for North and South America," Dorcas thought, "so it must not be on that side. E-U-R-," she spelled. "What comes after E-U-R-, Mother?"

"I have it," said Mary before Mother was able to answer.

"One more," Mother said. "The smallest continent is an island continent because it is completely surrounded by water. It is called **Australia** (ôˈstrāl•yə)."

"Aus tral ia," sounded Jonathan. Then he quickly pointed to Australia.

"The game is over," Mother said and smiled. "It looks as though— Oh, it is a tie. Both teams won."

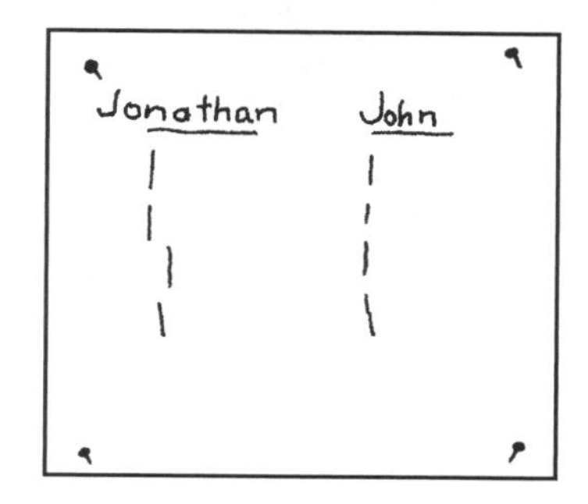

WRITING THE CONTINENT NAMES

Learn the names and locations of the seven continents as you do this exercise.

1. Write the names of the seven continents in the order that Mother named them for the geography match. If you do this correctly, you will have the largest continent first and the smallest continent last.

a. ______________________ e. ______________________

b. ______________________ f. ______________________

c. ______________________ g. ______________________

d. ______________________

2. On the map below, write the names of the continents on the correct lines. Use the map at the beginning of the story to help you.

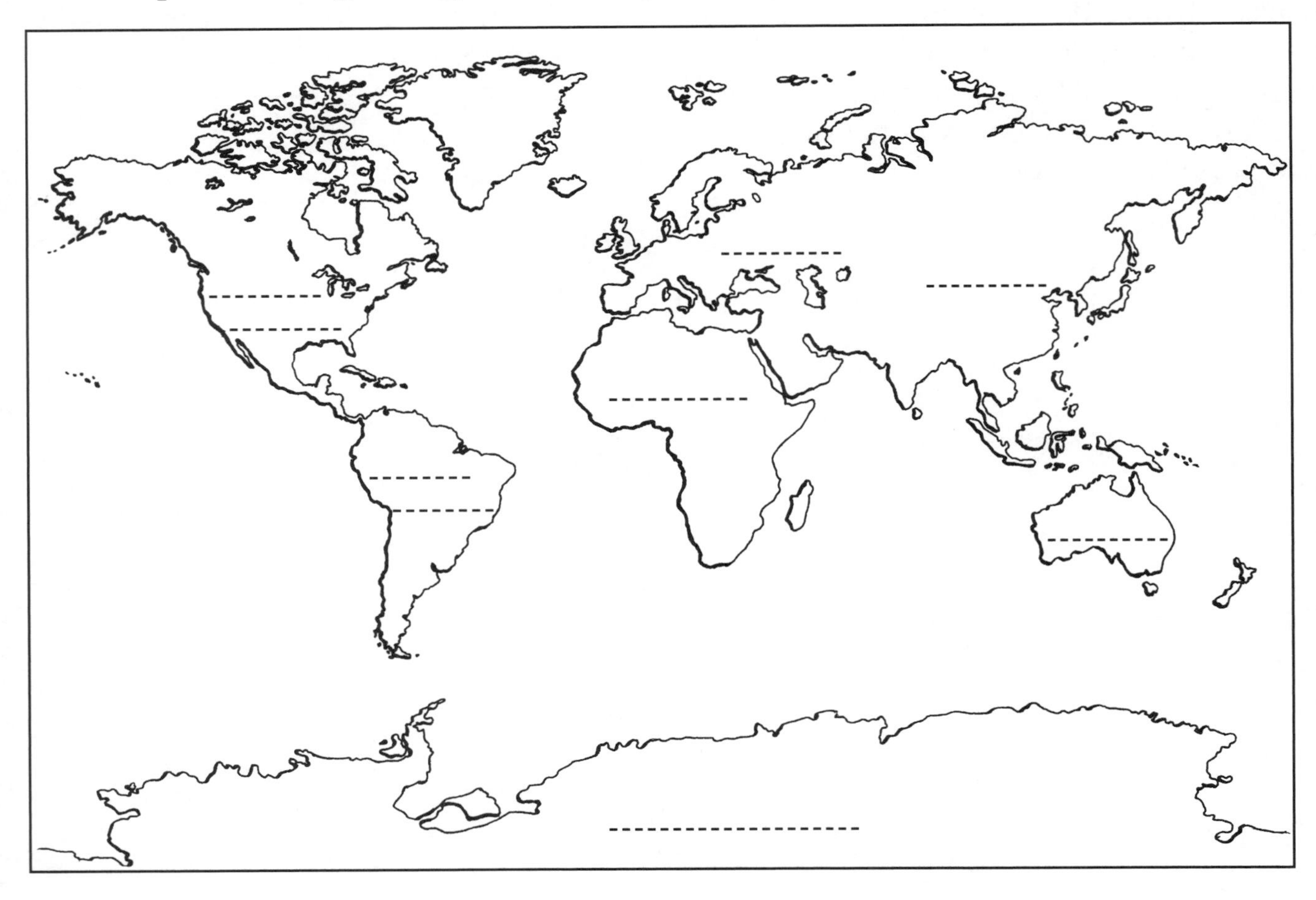

9. Directions on a Map

Below is a map of the world. Notice that the continents are not all in one straight line across the map. Some continents are near the top of the map, and some are close to the bottom. Some are near the right side of the map, and some are near the left side.

On every map, up is always north. Down is always south. To the left is always west, and to the right is always east.

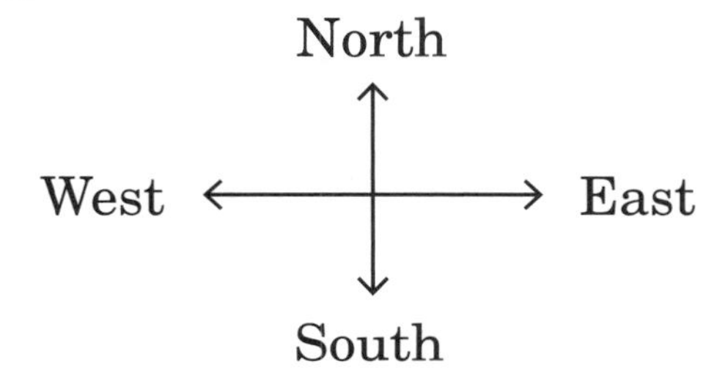

When we travel, we need to know which direction we want to go. Suppose we live in Ontario and want to travel to British Columbia. If we go east, we will get farther and farther from British Columbia. If we go north or south, we will not get there either. British Columbia is to the left of Ontario on a map; this shows us we will need to go west.

On the map, find the continent where you live. Perhaps your teacher will help you find the exact area where you live.

If you live in North America, which direction would you go to get to South America? Since South America is below North America on the map, you would go south.

Which direction would you go to get to Europe? Europe is to the right of North America, so you would go east.

Find Africa. Next, find Europe. Which direction is Africa from Europe? South is the answer, since Africa is below Europe on the map.

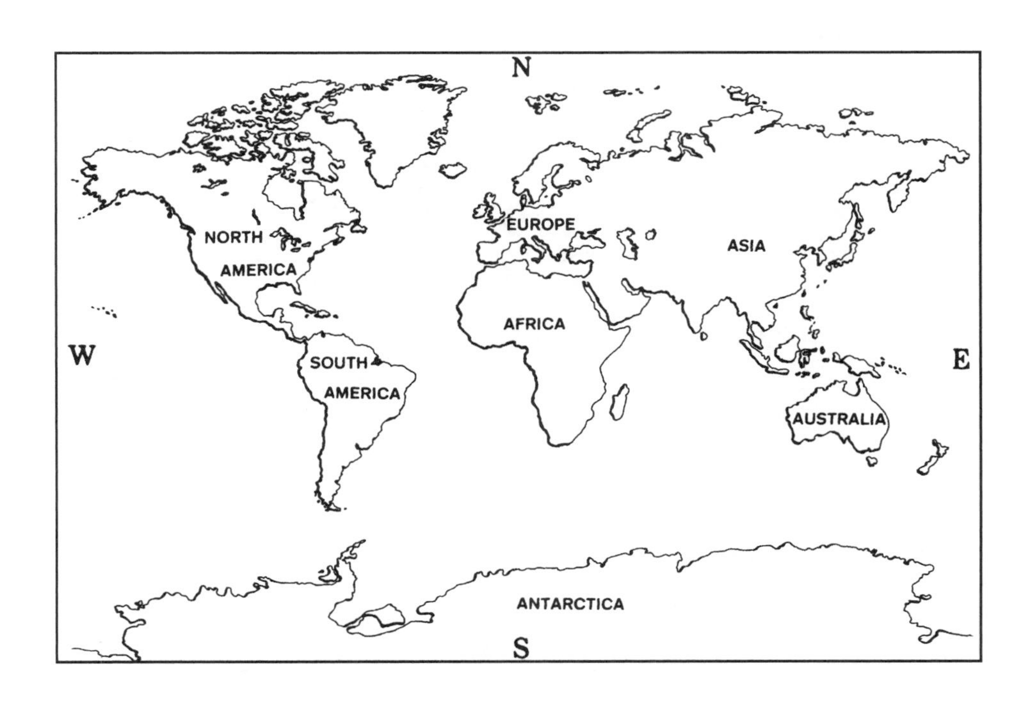

LEARNING DIRECTIONS ON A MAP

Answer these questions by looking at a large world map. Use a globe for number 6.

1. Which direction is Europe from North America? ____________________
2. Which direction is South America from Australia? ____________________
3. Which direction is Europe from Asia? ____________________
4. Which direction is Africa from Europe? ____________________
5. Which direction is South America from Africa? ____________________
6. Which direction is Antarctica from Australia? ____________________

Write the directions on a map.

7. N stands for north, S for south, E for east, and W for west. Write N, S, E, and W in the correct places on the map below.

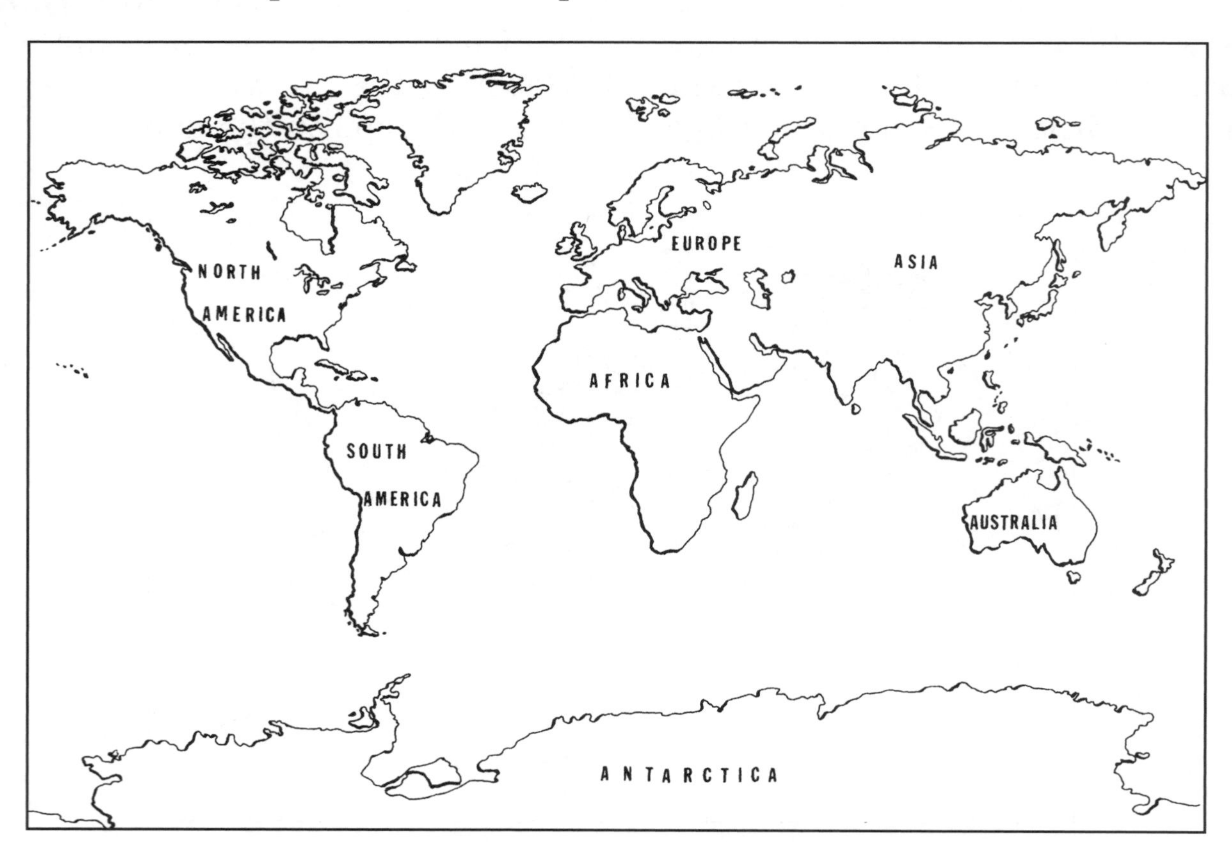

10. Oceans of the World

"Father, I like watching the waves of this ocean (ˈō•shən)," Dorcas shouted to be heard. Father, John, and Dorcas were standing on a rock, looking across the water. "Some of the waves are so high it seems they might climb this cliff and reach us. But the little ones can hardly reach the shore. Do the waves ever stop moving?"

"Oceans are not still like lakes are," Father told her. "The waves of the ocean always beat against the shore."

"If we would climb to a higher spot on the cliff, would we see land across the ocean?" asked John.

"No," said Father. "This ocean is so large that you could not see across it from the highest cliff or mountain peak. Do you know the song that goes like this?

'Wide, wide as the ocean,
High as the heaven above:
Deep, deep, as the deepest sea
Is my Saviour's love.
Though I'm so unworthy,
Yet I'm a child of His care;
For His Word teaches me
That His love reaches me
everywhere.' "

"Yes," John and Dorcas said together. "You taught it to us one time."

"Do you see that black speck?"

A ship on the ocean.

Father asked. "It is a large ship."

"I see it," they both said.

"That ship is going to a land across the ocean. It will sail for days before it reaches land," Father explained.

"Oh!" John exclaimed. "The ocean must be large."

"This ocean is the **Pacific** (pə'sif•ik) **Ocean**," Father told them. "It is the largest and deepest ocean, but there are three more oceans. The second largest ocean is the **Atlantic** (at'lan•tik) **Ocean.** The third largest is the **Indian** ('in•dē•ən) **Ocean.** The coldest ocean is the **Arctic** ('ärk•tik) **Ocean.** It is frozen most of the year. Very few people live near this ocean."

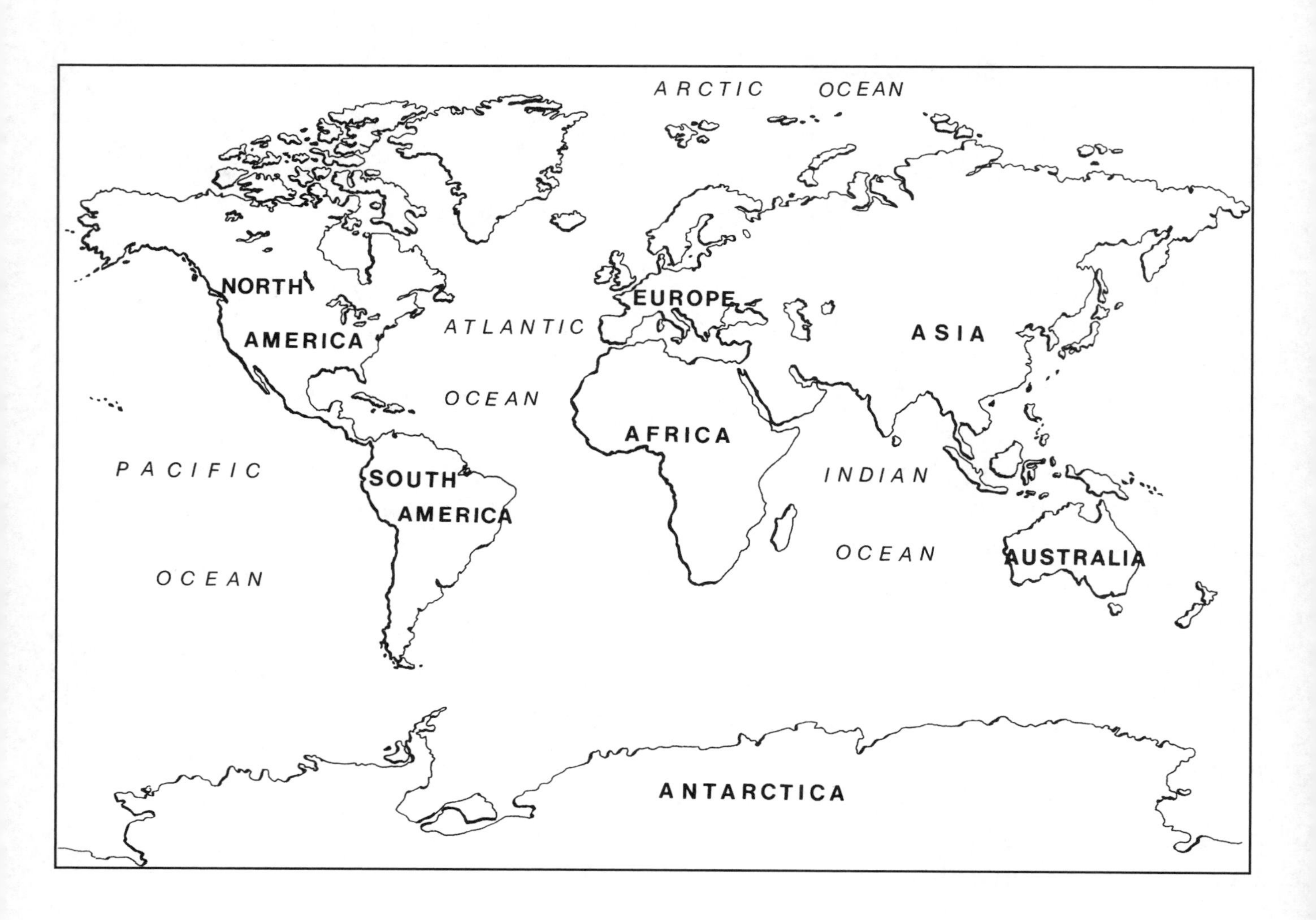

LEARNING THE OCEAN NAMES

Learn the names of the oceans and their locations as you do these exercises.

1. Below is a map of the world. Write the names of the four oceans in the correct places on the map.

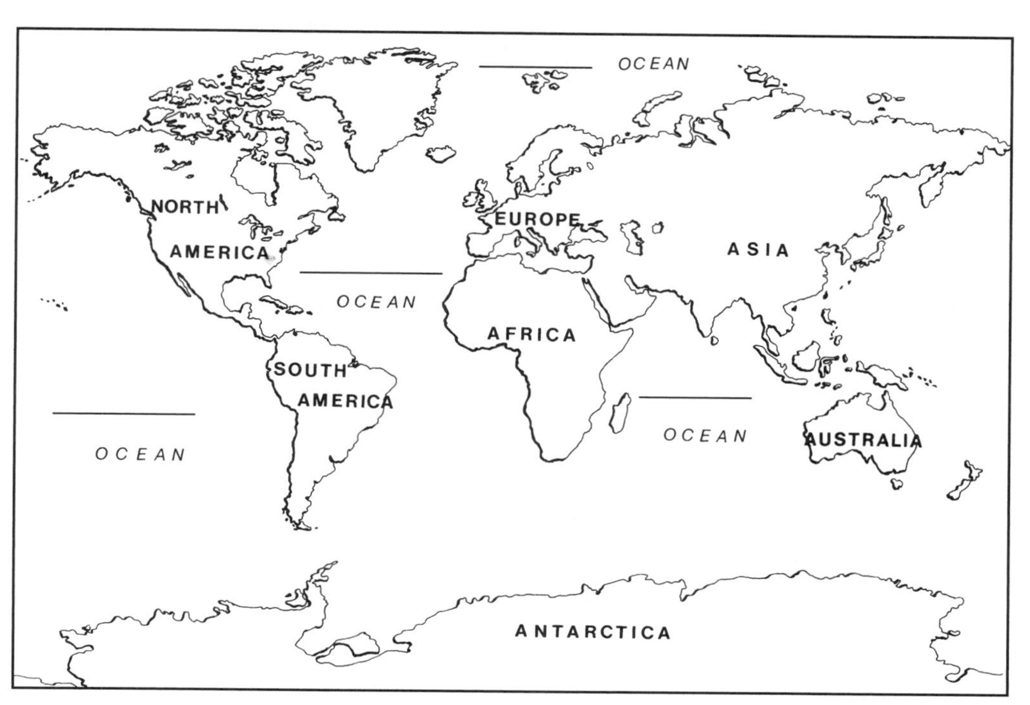

2. Which ocean is the largest? ______________________

3. Name the coldest ocean. ______________________

4. Name the third largest ocean. ______________________

5. Name the second largest ocean. ______________________

6. Name the ocean that is frozen most of the year. ______________________

7. Name the deepest ocean. ______________________

8. What can travel on oceans? ______________________

9. Name the oceans that touch the coasts of the continent in which you live.

______________________ ______________________ ______________________

11. Coloring Maps

Maps should be colored carefully. Colored marks in blue water that do not belong may cause someone to think there is a small island on the map that really is not there.

A map that is smoothly colored looks neat while a map that shows pencil streaks looks sloppy.

To make the coloring smooth, hold your pencil at a low angle and color lightly. This prevents lines from being seen on a map.

All oceans, seas, and lakes should be colored light blue so the border between land and water can be seen clearly.

MAP EXERCISES

Follow the directions above as you color these maps.

1. On the following map of North America, color Canada red, United States green, Mexico yellow, and Central America orange. Color the surrounding water light blue. Label the countries.

2. On this world map color North America green, South America light brown, Europe yellow, Asia red, Africa orange, Australia purple, and leave Antarctica white. Color the water light blue. Label the continents and oceans.

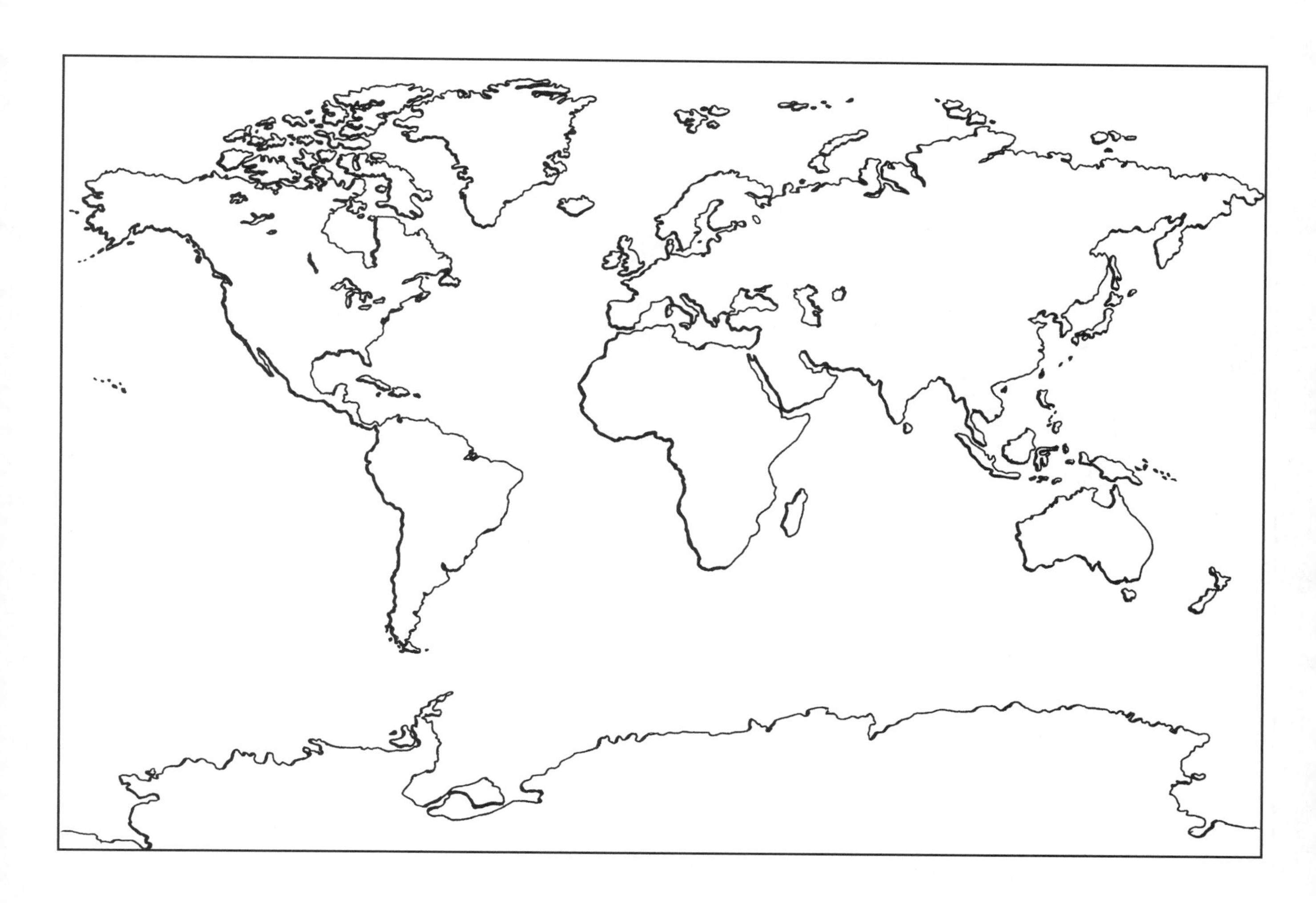

12. Review

Mark the 7 continents, 4 oceans, and 4 directions in the correct places on the following map. Then color North America purple, South America yellow, Asia orange, Europe green, Africa red, Australia pink, Antarctica white, and the oceans blue.

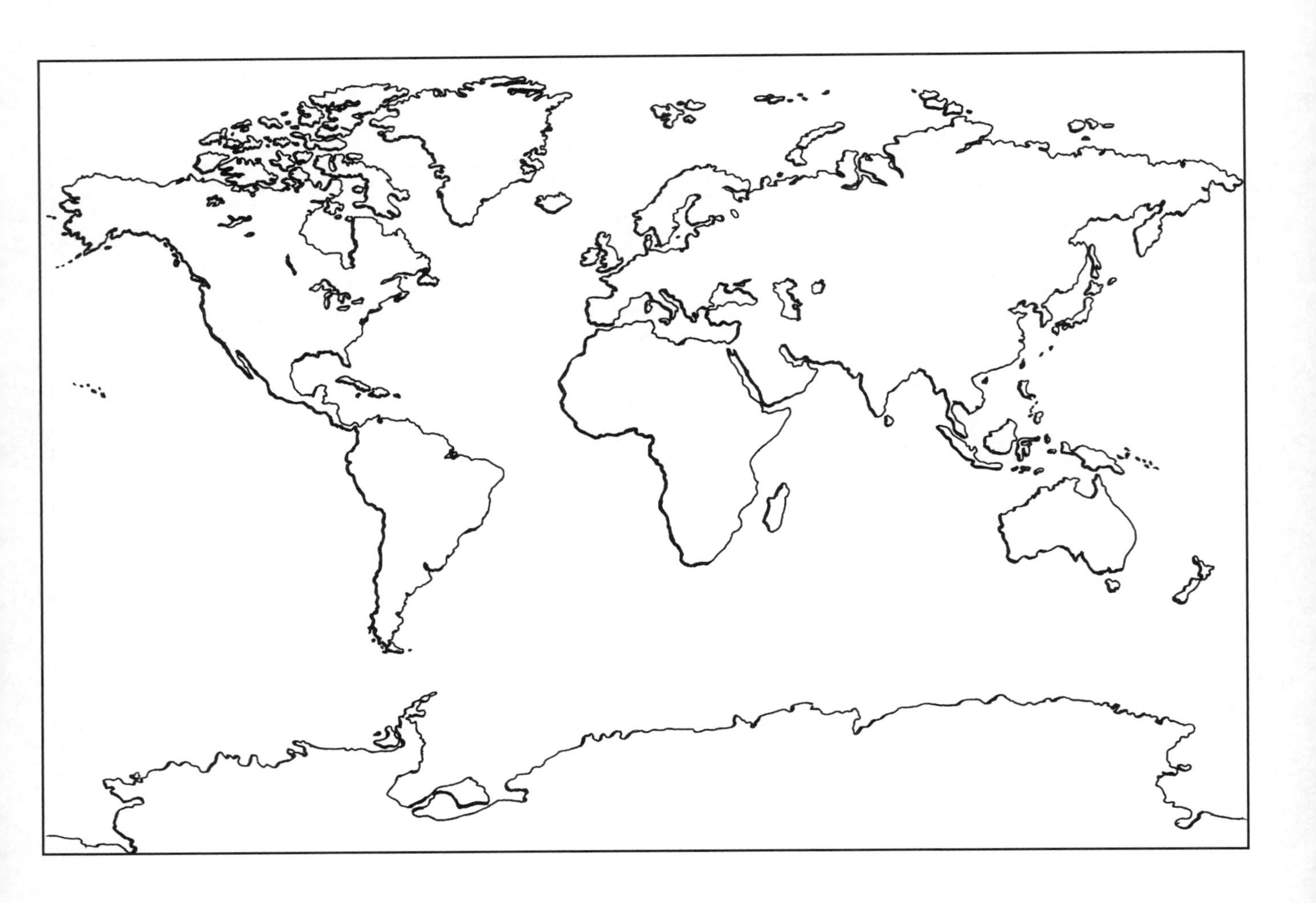

This is my Father's world—
The birds their carols raise;
The morning light, the lily white,
Declare their Maker's praise.

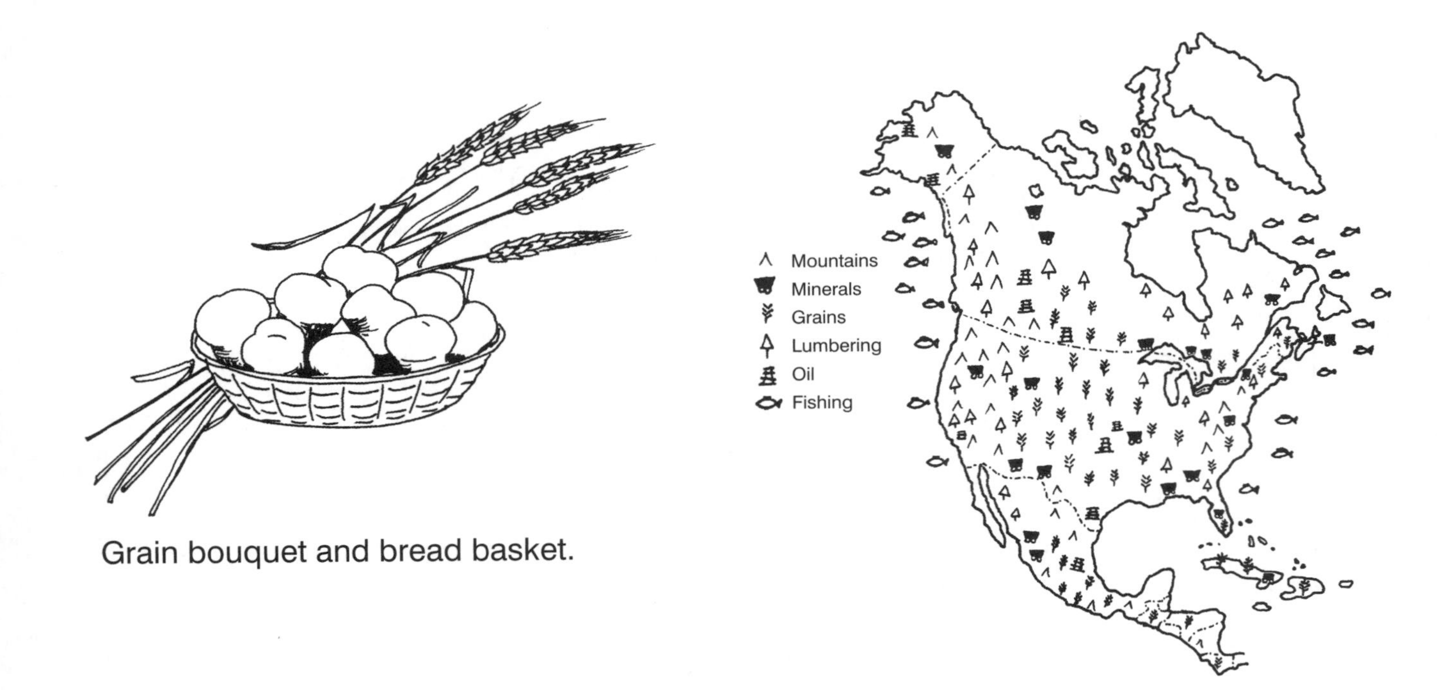

Grain bouquet and bread basket.

13. John of North America

"North America is divided into ten countries," Sister Esther, John's teacher, explained. "The three largest North American countries are Canada, the United States, and Mexico."

The summer holidays had ended, and John was again in the classroom. He listened carefully. He knew where all those places were on the map. But what was Sister Esther saying now?

"The central part of Canada and the United States is an important grain-growing area. Saskatchewan is called the **breadbasket** ('bred'bas•kit) of Canada; and Kansas is called the breadbasket of the United States," she said, pointing to the places on the map.

"Why would land be called a breadbasket?" John wondered with a puzzled look.

"They are called the breadbasket," she went on, "because of the grains that grow there. Bread is made from grains such as wheat and rye. Other grains such as barley, corn, and oats are sometimes used. Here are drawings of wheat, oats, and barley."

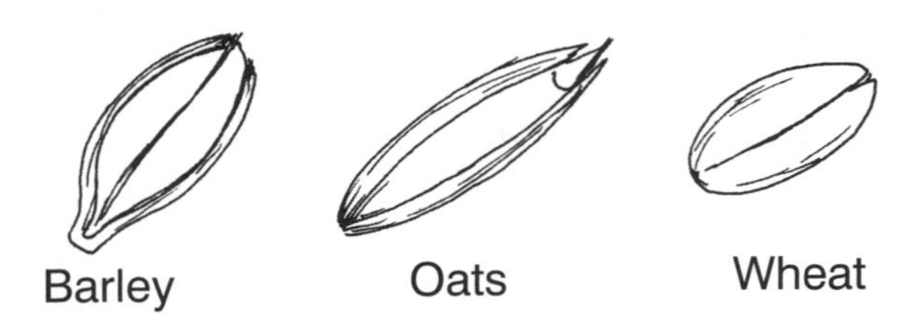

"Do farmers in North America grow enough grain to feed all their people?" Charles asked.

"Yes," answered Sister Esther. "They also sell some to other countries that do not have enough. North American farmers also raise many beef cattle for meat, and dairy cattle for milk, cheese, and butter. Potatoes and many other vegetables are grown to feed the people.

"On the map of North America are pictures to show what work the people of North America do. Can you name some things that people do besides farming?"

"I see pictures of fish on the oceans," Paul offered.

"Yes, you are right," Sister Esther agreed. "Some people fish for a living."

"Some men probably work where the black carts are," one boy guessed.

"The black carts stand for **minerals** (ˈmin•ər•əlz) such as gold, iron, lead, and silver, which are taken from **mines** (mīnz) in the earth. The tall towers represent oil," Sister Esther explained.

"I see some trees," suggested a boy whose Father worked at a sawmill. "Men cut logs from the trees and then saw the logs at a sawmill to make lumber."

"You are right," Sister Esther nodded. "What do we use in school that is made from trees?"

"Desks," one girl offered.

"Paper and pencils," said another.

"You are both right," she replied.

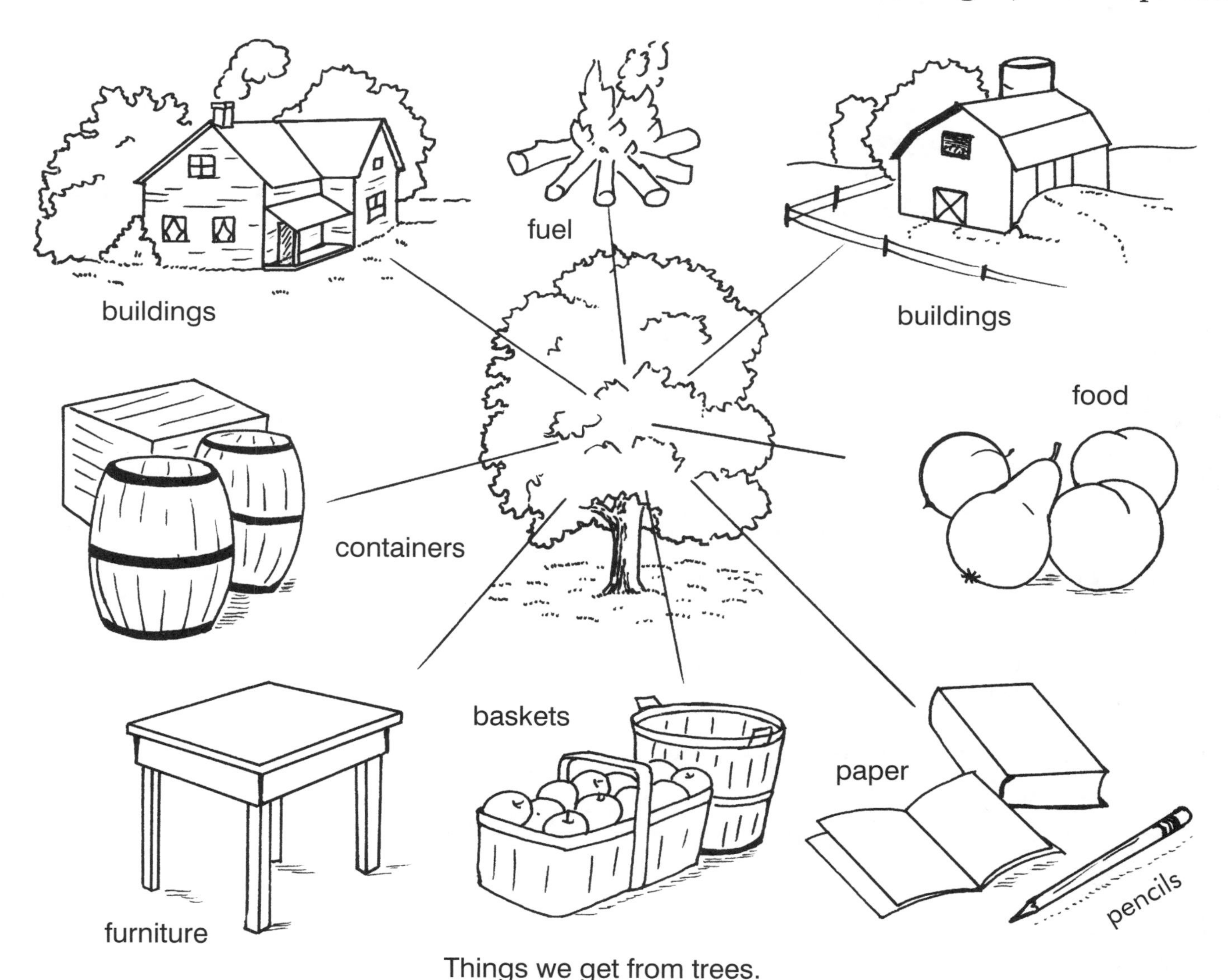

Things we get from trees.

"**Pulp** (pulp) and paper mills and furniture factories are scattered throughout the continent."

The class also discussed methods of travel and transportation.

"We travel to school in cars, vans, and buses," Gary said.

"If people want to go to distant places quickly, they travel by airplane," suggested another.

"Grain is hauled by trucks and trains," said Susan.

"Ships and airplanes are used to carry products to other continents," Sister Esther added. "In North America we have lots of good food, warm clothing, and well-built homes. People in some other continents don't have these privileges. We have much to be thankful for."

Car

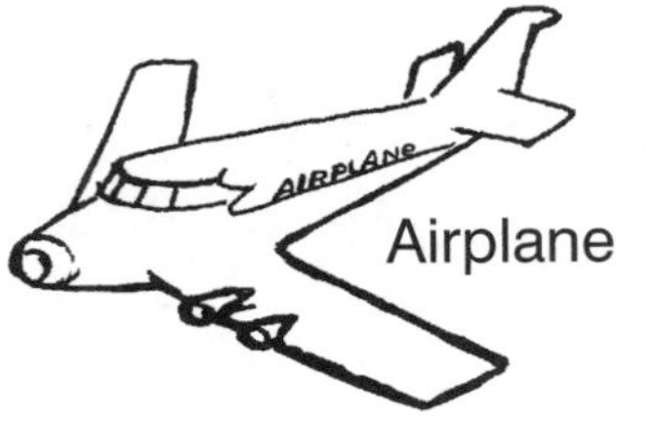

Airplane

Bus

Van

CROSSWORD PUZZLE

Fill in the crossword puzzle on the next page with words from the story.

Across

3. The number of large North American countries we have learned about.
5. Cheese and butter are made from the milk of these cows.
6. Places where logs are cut into lumber.
8. Important North American vegetables.
9. A kind of grain used to make bread.

Down

1. The kind of cows raised for meat.
2. The name given to Saskatchewan and Kansas because of the grain grown there.
4. The places from which minerals are taken.
7. A type of mineral.
8. It is made at pulp and paper mills.

1
2
3
4
5
6
7
8
9

14. Roberto of South America
Part 1

"Roberto (rō'ber•tō)," Mother called softly. "Time to get up."

Roberto rolled over on his wire mesh bed. He blinked his eyes as the light of the fire shone on him through the glassless window. He shifted his body as he tried to find a comfortable spot on his lumpy mattress.

"Good morning." Father smiled at him from the open doorway. "Breakfast will soon be ready."

Quickly Roberto folded his blanket and hurried outside. "Good morning Father and Mother!" he said as he walked toward the outdoor fire. "Are we having eggs this morning?" he asked as he noticed Mother pouring **soybean** ('soi'bēn) **oil** into a pan.

"Yes," Mother replied. "Father found these eggs on the ground by the **pineapple** ('pīn'ap əl) plant.

"Roberto," she continued as she cracked the egg and dropped it into the pan. "Push this stick into the fire. Watch that you don't touch the steel though. Father started the fire early so the steel is quite hot now."

"Soon I will need to leave for work. The sun will rise shortly," Father said after glancing at the eastern sky. "If I get my work done on time, tonight we will be able to go to prayer meeting."

"I'm glad the **Americano** (a'mār•ē•'kä nō) came to live near us," Roberto stated. "I like to hear him tell stories about Jesus."

"Yes," Father agreed. "Our neighbor is a kind man. He talks about a kind God, so maybe that is why he is so kind."

"Mother, what will I do today?" Roberto asked, looking at Mother.

"After you eat, you can fetch me a pail of water," Mother began with a smile. "Then we'll go down to the river and do our washing. But if you see a chicken before you get to the water, I want you to catch it so I can cook it for dinner. I'm glad I have a good worker, Father."

"I'm glad too," Father agreed.

"Mother," Father began. "I'll be hoeing today until I come home for a short sleep at **siesta** (sēˈes•tə). Do you need milk from our neighbor?"

"Yes," she replied. "And some flour to make **sopa** (ˈsō•pä—soup) for dinner tomorrow. I want to make **fiajaos** (fē•äˈzhounz—dark, reddish beans similar to kidney beans) with chicken today."

"It is time to go," Father stated as he placed his broad-brimmed **sombrero** (somˈbrär•ō) on his head. "It will be a hot day today."

Soon after Father was gone, Roberto started to the well for a pail of water. Just as he rounded the corner of their mud hut, he spied a chicken sitting between the **sunflowers** (ˈsunˈflou•ərz) and pineapples. "Just what Mother wants," he thought.

Quickly the little eight-year-old dropped his pail, and ran and grabbed the chicken before it had run very far between the plants. Just in time, he spied an egg lying on the ground.

"Mother, Mother," he called. "A chicken and an egg."

Roberto's mother looked up from stirring the beans in time to see the chicken give a jerk to try to escape Roberto's arms. "I'll take it and kill it for dinner," she said. "Push every piece of wood farther into the fire so it will be hot enough to cook the chicken."

A chicken between the sunflowers and pineapples.

Roberto quickly obeyed, being careful not to knock over the bricks that held up the steel rack where the pan of beans was sitting. Soon his bare feet were flying down the dusty path as he ran to fill the pail with water. Already his feet were nearly as red as the soil on which he ran. Soon he was back again, and then he and Mother set off for the river with their small load of garments to wash.

For Roberto, there was no school.

Roberto drawing water from a well.

"Maybe next year," Father had told him. "Our neighbor might start a **Spanish** (ˈspan•ish) school for boys and girls like you. If we have enough money to pay your way, maybe you can go then."

So when he saw eleven-year-old José (hōˈsā), with his **sling** (sling) in his hand, crossing the path ahead of them, he was not surprised. José had never been to school either. Instead, he was hunting a **parrot** (ˈpar•ət) so his mother could make soup. "Hello," Roberto called. José waved and smiled a friendly smile.

HOW WELL DO YOU REMEMBER?

Find a word in the story that names the following.

1. A South American bird that José was going to kill. ______________________
2. The Spanish word for dark, reddish beans. ______________________
3. The kind of oil Mother fried eggs in. ______________________
4. The kind of bed Roberto slept on. ______________________
5. What Father called their neighbors from the United States. ______________________
6. What Mother wanted Roberto to catch for dinner. ______________________
7. What José was hunting with. ______________________

Answer the following questions to tell where.

8. Where did Father find the eggs? ______________________
9. Where did Roberto get a pail of water? ______________________

10. Where was the chicken sitting? ______________________________

____

11. Where did Roberto find an egg? ______________________________

12. Where did Roberto and his mother go with the garments? ____________

____

13. Where was the pan of beans sitting? __________________________

14. Where did Roberto push the wood? ____________________________

Show how John's and Roberto's life are different by telling about each of these things.

	John's life	Roberto's life
15. Season	winter	summer
16. Breakfast	(your breakfast)	
17. School (Yes or No)		
18. Where Mother cooks		
19. What Mother cooks on		
20. Father's work		
21. Color of ground		
22. Type of house		

15. Roberto of South America Part 2

The sun rose higher and higher in the sky. Father wiped the sweat from his face as he stopped hoeing for a few moments. Row after row of bean plants were all around him. Most of the field was already hoed.

"Maybe I'll chop down some **jungle** (ˈjung•gəl) after siesta (a midday nap)," thought Father.

Just a short distance from Father, the jungle grew thick and tall. Quickly, he turned his head toward the nearest **palm** (päm) **tree.** "What was that?" he wondered.

Again a grunting sound came to him. Laying his hoe beside the bean plants, Father grabbed his gun that was lying nearby. The sound of a hungry **wild pig** came closer. Father raised his gun, ready to fire at the first glimpse of the pig's head as it came from between the trees.

Bang! The pig dropped to the ground. With his knife, Father cut the pig's throat so the blood would run out. After skinning the pig, he cut the meat into pieces. "By the time I carry this meat home, and get milk and flour from the neighbor, it will be time for siesta," he thought. "It is hot again this morning. Too hot for a man to work. After I eat and sleep, then I'll be ready to cut jungle."

As he walked toward home, carrying the milk and the flour, he noticed a donkey hitched to a

A cart loaded with bananas.

two-wheeled cart coming down the road. The cart was loaded with large bunches of **bananas** (bə'nan•əz). "Maybe Carlos ('kär•los) is going to sell them and buy a new pair of shoes for his wife, Juanita (wä'nē•tə)," he thought.

"Hello, Father," Mother and Roberto called from the doorway where they were sitting.

"Honk, honk!" A rattly bus slowed as it neared their mud hut. Father waved and shook his head. Understanding that no one wanted a ride, the bus driver did not stop, but hurried on his way.

"Tomorrow you should plan to go to town, Mother," Father said.

"All right," Mother replied. "The chicken and fiajaos are ready to eat now."

While they ate the slightly cooked chicken and fiajaos, Father told about killing the pig. "He was coming to eat beans in the field," Father explained. "We will share the meat with our neighbors. They will be glad to have some wild pig meat to eat."

While they were eating, they heard the sound of a large herd of cattle coming along the road. "Can you see the **cowboys** ('kou'boiz) on their horses yet?" Mother asked Roberto.

"Not yet," Roberto answered.

"They are probably from the cattle **ranch** (ranch)," Father said.

Slowly the cattle plodded nearer, mooing as they came. A number of cowboys were galloping beside and behind them, making sure the cattle stayed on the road. The cattle were

Cowboy herding cattle.

being moved to a different field.

After they had eaten, Mother gathered up the dishes to be washed later at the river. Father and Roberto laid on their beds where the hot sun could not beat on them. Mother picked some ripe oranges from a nearby tree for Father and Roberto when they woke up.

Orange tree

"I will waken them in the middle of the afternoon when the sun is not so hot," she thought. "Father will want to cut down the jungle with his **machete** (mə'shet•ē). By tonight I will have Father's and Roberto's clothes clean and ready for prayer meeting. I'm glad we can go again. I want to hear more about God."

SEEING HOW WELL YOU REMEMBER

Answer the following questions in complete sentences. See how many you can answer without looking back into the story.

1. Is a siesta a time to work or a time to rest? ____________________

____

2. Why did Father take a siesta in the middle of the day? ____________________

____

3. What was Father doing before he killed the pig? ____________________

____

4. What was Father going to do after siesta? ____________________

____

____

5. What did Father have with him that showed he was used to seeing wild animals when he was working? ____________________

____

6. What did Roberto's father plan to do with the pig when he got it home? ____

____

____

____

7. Where were the cowboys taking the cattle? ____________________

____

____

Fill in the blanks with the correct word or words from the story.

8. ________________ trees grew near the bean plants.

9. The animal that Father killed was a ________________.

10. Carlos was taking ________________ to town to sell.

11. Father bought ________________ and ________________ from the neighbor.

12. Father used a ________________ to cut down the jungle.

13. Men that look after large herds of cattle are called ________________.

14. Father, Mother and Roberto planned to go to ________________ that night.

15. Mother picked some ________________ from a tree for Father and Roberto to eat after they woke up.

16. For dinner the family had chicken and ________________.

16. Seebo of Asia
Part 1

Cock-a-doodle-doo rang through the small, mud house, waking the family at five o'clock in the morning.

Tinkle, tinkle. The **water buffalo's** (ˈbuf•ə•lōz) bell sounded as she walked outside from her room in the mud house.

Seebo (ˈsē•bō), an eight-year-old **tribal** (ˈtrī•bəl) **Indian** (ˈin•dē•ən) boy of India, lay quietly blinking and rubbing the sleep from his eyes. "I hope Loknath (ˈlock•nut) and Kartik (ˈkär•tik) can come along with us today to take care of the cattle," he thought as he heard the tinkling of the water buffalo's bell.

Cluck, cluck, cluck, came from behind him. The chickens were rising with the early morning sun and were eagerly running toward the light. *Whir-r-r!* A chicken landed softly on the ground in front of Seebo and quickly ran out the door. Others followed close behind.

Quickly Mother, Father, and Seebo arose. After bathing, Mother cleaned her teeth and began her morning duties. Father went outside to milk the water buffalo.

Swish, swish went the straw broom as Mother carefully swept the

Straw broom

house, yard, and road in front of the yard.

"A hard-working wife I have," Father said as he set the bowl of milk down and reached for the water Mother had carried in.

"Here's your twig, Father," Seebo said as he brought Father a twig to clean his teeth.

Soon Father was finished bathing, and it was Seebo's turn.

"Thank you for the twig, Seebo," Father said as he picked it up. After chewing on the end of the twig, he began to vigorously brush his shining, white teeth and his tongue until his mouth was clean and fresh.

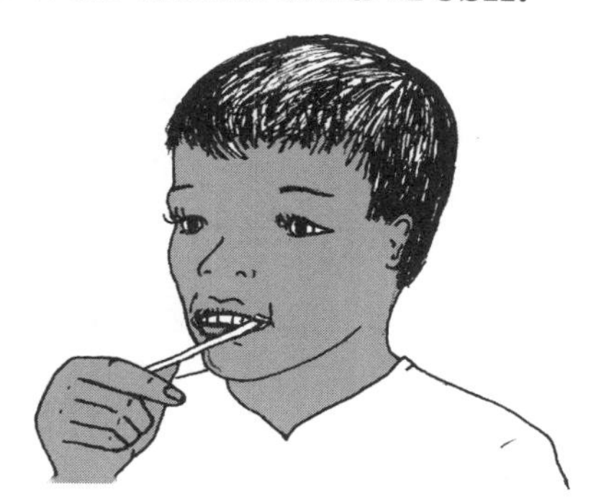

Brushing teeth with a twig.

"Lucknow (ˈluk•nou), come to Father" Father tenderly called his little son and then gently lifted him and held him close. He then stepped out of their house into the outdoors.

"Is the rice almost cooked, Mother?" Father questioned as he bent down and pushed the wood farther into the low fire.

"Yes, it is finished now," Mother replied. She lifted the hot pot of rice from the fire, using large leaves for potholders. Tipping the pot of rice,

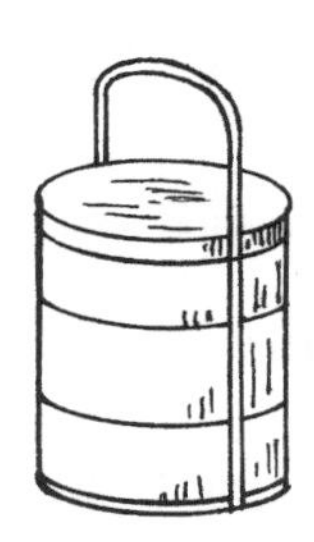

Dekchee—a sectioned lunch pail.

she began filling Father's **dekchee** (ˈdek•chē—lunch pail). "Where will you plow today, Father?" she questioned.

"In one of the little fields by the river," Father replied. "The farmer will tell us where to plow when we get there."

Just then a clean and smiling Seebo came up to where Father and Mother were standing. "Is the rice ready for my lunch?" he wondered.

"Yes. It is already in your dekchee. The shepherd, Dhamau (dəˈmä), will soon go by," Mother said smilingly.

"Here they come," Seebo said, looking down the road. "I must leave now." He quickly went for his stick and then picked up his dekchee and **safee** (ˈsaf•ē—a cotton, towel-like, shoulder piece).

TESTING YOUR UNDERSTANDING

Find the answer in the story, and write it on the blanks below.

1. The family was awakened in the morning by the crowing of a ____________________.
2. ____________________ is the Indian name for a (sectioned) lunch pail.
3. Father went outside to milk the ____________________________.
4. The family arose at ____________________ in the morning.

5. Mother used a ________________________ to brush her teeth.

6. She used a ________________________ to sweep the house.

7. Mother used ________________________ for potholders.

8. Seebo lives in a country called ________________________.

9. He is ______________________ years old.

10. The food that Seebo eats for dinner is ________________________.

Find the part at the right to complete the sentence at the left, and write the letter on the line.

___	11.	Mother did her cooking	a. went with the shepherd, Dhamau.
___	12.	Father was going to plow	b. in the house.
___	13.	Each day Seebo	c. on an outdoor fire.
___	14.	His job was	d. to help look after the cattle.
___	15.	The water buffalo slept	e. in a small field by the river.

The tribal Indian people are a clean people. Find three examples of cleanliness in this story.

16. a. ____

b. ____

c. ____

Name three things that Seebo took with him when he went with Dhamau.

17. a. __________________________

b. __________________________

c. __________________________

17. Seebo of Asia
Part 2

"Good morning," Seebo sang out as he saw the boys, sticks in hands, coming behind a herd of cows. Slowly he walked behind their own water buffalo as it joined the herd.

"Good morning," they all greeted Seebo.

Down the village road they went. Other boys with their water buffaloes joined in with the group as they went through the village.

As they reached the edge of the village, the boys moved up beside the cattle to make sure they would not stray into one of the rice fields beside the road, but would enter the right pasture.

Boys herding water buffalo.

As the cattle grazed, the old shepherd, Dhamau, seated himself on a rock, keeping his eyes on the cows to make sure they did not wander too close to the rice fields.

"The last rains of the season are over," the shepherd said. "Magrundoo's (maˈgrun•dōōz) crop is ready to be harvested."

"Harvest will begin this week in our fields too," Cheta (ˈchē•tä) commented. "Father built a hut near the rice fields. My brother will stay in the hut this year to guard the crop so no one will steal it."

"You won't be able to help take care of the cattle then, will you?" Dhamau commented.

"No, Grandma said she will come

instead of me," said Cheta.

"Cutting and hauling the rice will keep you busy for a couple of days," Dhamau stated, picking up his stick.

"Father wants to begin cleaning the threshing floor when he comes home tonight," Cheta told them. "Father sharpened Mother's and the girls' sickles. In three days Mother and the girls will begin cutting the rice. I am looking forward to helping Father haul the rice and stack it near the threshing floor."

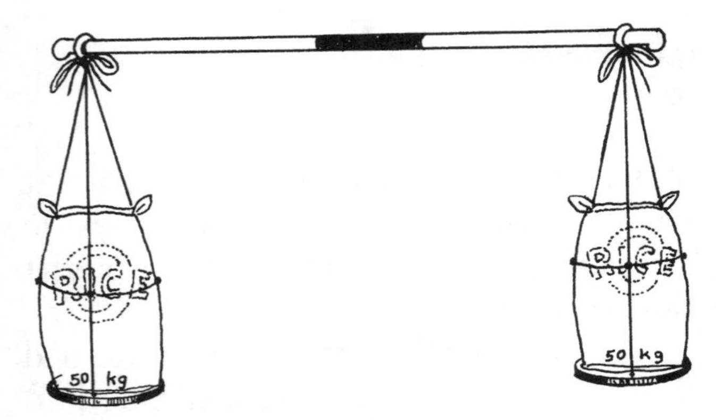

Jilkies are used by men to carry bundles of rice.

"The cows!" Cheta shouted excitedly, pointing to the rice fields that the cattle were nearing.

"Khed! Khed! (Chase! Chase!)" Dhamau waved his stick toward the cows, and the boys were off in a flash to keep the cows from entering the rice field.

The boys soon had the cows headed toward a nearby water hole. In a short time, all that could be seen of the water buffaloes was the tops of their heads sticking out of the water.

Soon it was dinnertime. Dhamau

Water buffaloes

and the boys fingered the rice from their dekchees. The hot sun beat down on them, causing the sweat to run from their faces.

"Tell us a story," Vilas urged Dhamau.

"Did you hear about the fox that fell into a well?" Dhamau asked.

"A fox in a well?" Janglee exclaimed. "What did the people do?"

"The farmer made a snare and caught the fox in it," Dhamau answered.

"What's a snare?" Seebo questioned.

"A snare is a loop tied at the end of a rope," Dhamau told them. "The farmer let the rope down into the well until the loop touched the water. When the fox swam into the loop, the farmer pulled on the rope, and the loop fastened around the fox's neck. When he got the fox out, he killed it."

The rest of the afternoon the boys spent looking for **puff balls,** at the same time watching so that the cows did not wander into the rice fields.

At six o'clock they headed for home. Each cow knew its home and turned into its own yard while the others plodded down the road.

Supper was at eight o'clock. Mother dished out the rice mixed with mustard greens and topped with sweet-smelling **curry** ('kûr•ē).

"Um-m-m," thought a tired Seebo. "How delicious!"

Supper was soon over, and the family prepared for bed.

Curry on rice

TESTING YOUR UNDERSTANDING

On the line following the description, write the name of the person or thing that is described.

1. Dhamau and the boys carry me in their hand and use me to chase the water buffalo out of the rice. ____________________

2. The only part of the buffaloes' bodies that was sticking out of the water.

____

3. The crop that grew in the fields that the cattle were not to enter. __________

4. The boys hunted for me in the afternoon. ____________________

5. What the boys used to eat their rice with at dinner. ____________________

6. It was mixed in the rice for supper. ____________________________

7. It was placed on top of the rice. __________________

Find answers in the story for these questions about the tribal Indian people.

8. Do the farmers begin harvesting their crops before the last rains of the season or after the last rains of the season? ____________________________

____

9. Why did Father build a hut near the rice fields? ______________________________

10. Who will help take care of the cattle while Cheta helps his father haul the rice to the threshing floor? ______________________________

11. When did the people in the story go to bed? ______________________________

18. Review

Tell in which continent or continents (North America, South America, or Asia) you learned about each of these events.

1. Mother regularly cooks on an outdoor fire (two continents). ____________________ ____________________
2. Wheat is grown. ____________________
3. Rice is grown. ____________________
4. Father hoes beans and cuts down the jungle. ____________________
5. The breadbasket is in the central part of the continent. ____________________
6. Boys help take care of water buffalo. ____________________
7. Boys hunt parrots with a sling. ____________________
8. Father drives the children to school in a car. ____________________
9. Father takes a siesta in the middle of the day. ____________________
10. Mother uses a straw broom to sweep the floor, yard, and road in front of the house. ____________________

Fill in each blank with the correct word from one of the stories.

11. Materials such as gold and silver that are taken from a mine are called ____________________.
12. Roberto's father wears a ____________________ to protect his head from the hot sun.

13. The lunch pail that Seebo carries his food in is called a ______________.

14. Roberto's father uses a ______________ to cut down the jungle.

15. Seebo uses a __________ to brush his teeth.

Draw a picture below of something you learned about in this chapter. See if your classmates can guess what the picture is about.

16.

His hand the wonders wrought.

19. Antarctica

"It's a cold morning," Father said to John as he stepped outside the door and took a breath of the frosty air. Their steps made a loud, crunching sound as they walked over the hard-packed snow to the car.

"Today we're going to have geography," John told Father as they drove out the lane. "Sister Esther said we will learn about another continent today. The continent's name starts like *Ant* but I can't say it."

"Antarctica," Father said for him. "Today would remind you of Antarctica."

"Why?" John questioned.

"It's white and cold here just like it is in Antarctica," Father replied.

"Then they must be having winter too," John concluded.

"No, not really," Father replied. "Antarctica is a continent that is covered with an **ice sheet** all year round. Today it is summer there. But the temperature never gets very warm in Antarctica."

The car slowed down as it pulled up to the school. "Good-by, Father," John said as he hopped out.

"Good-by, John," Father replied. "Have a good day."

The day passed quickly, and soon it was time for geography class.

"Who remembers what continent we are going to learn about today?" Sister Esther asked as she picked up the globe and walked to the front of the room.

Many eager hands shot up. "Antarctica," a girl near the front of the room answered.

"Did anyone try to find where it is on the globe?" Sister Esther asked.

Paul had, and going to the front, he pointed to an area near the bottom of the globe.

"What color is Antarctica on the globe?" she asked, turning the globe on its side so everyone could see. "Yes, John?" she asked as his hand went up.

"White," John replied.

"Do you know why it is white, John?" Sister Esther asked.

"It is covered with an ice sheet all year long," he answered.

"That's right," Sister Esther agreed. "An ice sheet is a thick layer of ice and snow. In many places this sheet of ice is over 1 kilometer (over one-half mile) thick. Mountains stick out through the ice sheet in the center of Antarctica and along the coast.

"Antarctica is a very lonely continent. No one lives there. A number of stations have been set up and men visit the continent for short periods of time to study the weather, ice sheet, and forms of life on the continent.

"The largest land creature they have found is a wingless fly that looks like a housefly and is less than 3 millimeters (about one-eighth inch) long. A number of smaller insects make their home here.

"Because of the deep sheet of snow and the extreme cold, there is very little plant life in Antarctica. Only hardy plants such as **lichens** (ˈlī•kənz), **mosses** (ˈmôs•əz), and two kinds of grasses grow on the few rocky hillsides.

"The most unusual Antarctic bird is the **penguin** (ˈpen•gwin). It is a very unusual bird that stands on short legs and walks with a clumsy waddle. Penguins cannot fly, but they are very good swimmers. They eat fish.

"The Antarctic waters abound with fish. They are also the home of seals and whales."

"Is the water around Antarctic frozen all year long?" John asked.

"During the summer the sun warms the water in the nearby ocean and the ice breaks up into large chunks called **icebergs** (ˈīs•bûrgz)," Sister Esther explained.

"Antarctica wouldn't be a very nice place to live, would it?" another boy questioned.

"No," Sister Esther assured him. "No food can grow on Antarctica. The air is very dry and cold. Strong winds blow across the land, carrying the snow with them. Some of the early explorers froze to death on Antarctica. Yet God has provided some forms of plant and animal life that can live even in that cold land."

Seals resting on a large chunk of ice. Smaller icebergs are in the background.

HOW WELL DO YOU REMEMBER?

Underline the correct answer or answers to these questions.

1. Which of the following animals do not live on or near the Antarctic seacoast?

   a. seals b. whales c. polar bears d. penguins

2. Which of these plants grow on the rocky hillsides? (Find two.)

   a. trees b. mosses c. vegetables d. lichens

3. The air in Antarctica is very (Give two).

   a. warm b. moist c. dry d. cold

4. The largest land creature in Antarctica looks like a

   a. housefly b. bird c. fish d. lichen

5. Large chunks of ice that break off and float in the water are called

   a. ice caps b. snow balls c. icicles d. icebergs

6. The thick layer of ice and snow on Antarctica is called an

   a. ice flow b. ice cap c. iceberg d. ice sheet

Answer these questions.

7. Why does no one live on Antarctica? ______________________________

   ____

8. On what part of the globe is Antarctica located? ____________________

   ____

9. What is the name of a bird that spends most of its time in the ocean? ______

   ____

10. For what reasons do men visit and spend some time on Antarctica? ______

    ____

Color the pictures in this lesson.

Penguins under the southern lights along a rocky shore in Antarctica.

20. Maria of Europe

"Maria, see if Grandmother is ready for family worship," Mother requested as she set the bacon and eggs in the oven to keep warm.

Eight-year-old Maria skipped toward Grandmother's bedroom, knocked, and then quietly waited until she heard Grandmother cheerfully call, "Come in, Maria."

As Maria opened the door, she noticed Grandmother's Bible lying open on the bed. "Grandmother!" she exclaimed. "Some **officers** (ˈô•fə•sərz) passed by our house this morning. One just passed on his motorcycle as I came from the kitchen. They frighten me, Grandmother."

Maria talking to Grandmother.

"Trust in God," Grandmother encouraged her. "But I'm glad you told me, for I will need to hide my Bible. Please take this cup to the kitchen, and tell Mother I will come to the worship room soon. Do not talk about the Bible to just anyone, remember, because your Father is already in danger."

Czechoslovakia (ˈchek•ə•slōˈvä•kē ə), the country where the Charvat (ˈshär•vət) family live, is in the communist part of Europe. The leaders do not believe in God, and they make it hard for all who do.

Mr. Charvat is a minister whom the officers are watching very closely. It is dangerous for the family to worship openly. This morning before breakfast, as usual, they secretly gathered in their tiny worship room to read the Bible and pray together.

At other times, Grandmother reads from the Bible to Maria and her brothers, Josef (ˈyō•sef) and Janick (ˈyän•ik), in their worship room. Before they begin reading, Grandmother always pulls the door tightly shut.

After family worship, the family gathered in the kitchen for breakfast. Thankfully, they sat down to a good breakfast. Maria took a sip of her warm **chi** (chī)—**chicory** (ˈchik•ər•ē) tea. Mother always added milk to the children's chi.

"Is your homework finished?" Mother asked.

"Yes," the children chorused. They knew they must have their homework done. Each morning Teacher would look at their books soon after school began. If someone did not have his homework done, the other children were not allowed to talk to him or even look at him that day. Maria never wanted to enter the classroom without having her homework done.

"I have not had a mark against me yet this year," Maria told Mother.

"Father and I do not want you to either, Maria," Mother reminded her. "It could be very serious for Father if Teacher would send a note home with you because of uncompleted homework or bad behavior."

On this warm March morning, Father had to leave very early to work on the farm. No excuse would ever be listened to if he were late. Because Father was from a Christian home, he had not been allowed to advance in school beyond grade five. After he was out of school, the **authorities** (əˈthôr•ə•tēz) had told him where he must work. Any misbehavior or lack of diligence by him or his family would be considered sufficient reason by the authorities to punish Father.

Before Maria left for school, she went to her bedroom and knelt down and prayed, "Dear kind Father in heaven, keep me safe from danger today. Help me to be brave when the boys and girls at school laugh at Jesus or make fun of my parents because they are Christians. Please help me to be good and to do my work well. In Jesus' Name. Amen."

Maria asking God's protection.

Soon Maria and her brothers were on the road, bicycling toward school. Maria's brothers lovingly stayed close to her so she would be protected from bad boys. They passed large orchards of peaches and plums, which were just beginning to bud. Apple and pear trees were in full blossom.

The sound of a motorcycle approaching caused fear to well up in Maria's heart. Soon an officer appeared, and as he passed them, a look of scorn crossed his face. "Christians," he muttered scornfully when he noticed that they were not wearing a red scarf around their necks. To the children's relief, he quickly passed on.

The children leaned their bicycles against the fence just inside the gate and then hurried to the corner of the school yard, where some children from Christian homes were playing. Each day they were shunned and mocked by the children from non-Christian homes.

When the bell rang, the children filed quietly into the classroom. On the walls were pictures of the country's leader, and also of the leader of **Russia** (ˈrush•ə). Everyone was required to learn the Russian language. Many times during the day, the teacher told them how great their leaders were. But Maria, her brothers, and the other children from Christian homes often prayed, "Dear God, help me to always remember how wonderful You are. Help me never to believe that men are greater than You."

After school, Maria and her brothers quickly hurried home to escape the teasing and mocking of the other children. It was always a relief to arrive home safely each night.

"I'm so glad to be safely at home," Maria said as she entered the house.

"We're glad you're home safely too." Mother and Grandmother nodded agreement from their chairs where they were doing hand sewing.

Maria got her sewing and sat down

Maria and Grandmother sewing.

with them. She had learned to sew by watching Mother and Grandmother closely and carefully when they were sewing.

That evening a tired but happy Father returned home with a parcel of cheese, butter, and meat from the farm. As they sat down to their supper of homemade soup, potatoes, chicken, and vegetables, a sincere prayer of thanksgiving was offered that Father had again returned home safely.

The family at the table.

LEARNING ABOUT CZECHOSLOVAKIA

Write the answers to these questions on the lines.

1. In what continent is Czechoslovakia? ____________________
2. What did Grandmother Charvat have that needed to be kept hidden? ____________________
3. Who was watching Father closely? ____________________
4. Whom did Grandmother tell Maria to trust in? ____________________
5. In what room did the family read the Bible? ____________________
6. What is the name of the tea they drink in Czechoslovakia? ____________________
7. What did Maria and her brothers not wear that showed the officer they were children from a Christian home? ____________________
8. Who made fun of children from Christian homes? ____________________ ____________________
9. What language was everyone expected to learn? ____________________
10. Name four kinds of fruit trees given in the story. ____________________ ____________________ ____________________ ____________________
11. What pictures were on the walls of the school? ____________________ ____________________
12. Where did Father work? ____________________
13. What three foods did he bring home? ____________________ ____________________ ____________________

Write the answers to these questions in well-worded sentences.

14. Why did the family worship in a secret room? ______________________

____

____

15. Find one proof that Maria was taught respect. ______________________

____

16. For what reason were some children held back from going beyond grade five in school? ______________________

____

17. What happened if someone did not have his homework done? ______________________

____

18. Why was Father's safe arrival home such a concern to the family? ______________________

____

21. Kathryn of Australia

March winds gently blew around the Fitzgerald family as they walked among the tall gum trees in south Australia.

"Look, Mother!" Kathryn exclaimed, tugging at her mother's arm and pointing up into a nearby **eucalyptus** (ˈyo͞o•kəˈlip•təs) tree. "There is a little animal in that tree."

"That looks like a **koala** (kōˈä•lə) eating its favorite meal, eucalyptus leaves," Mother explained, watching the little animal with interest. "Father, is the koala's cub climbing up the mother's back?"

"Yes, I believe it is," Father smilingly replied. "It probably was in her **pouch** (pouch) and is getting hungry too. The koala cub is having a horseback ride."

Mother and Kathryn joined Father in laughter. Their laughter was cut short, however, by a loud laughing call that pierced the air. This was followed by another similar sound.

Scott and Andrew, who had run a short distance ahead, came running back. "Father!" they exclaimed, "Was that a **kookaburra** (ˈko͝ok•əˈbûr•ə)?"

Kookaburra

"The first sounded like a kookaburra, but the second was Australia's **imitator** (ˈim•əˈtā•tər)," Father told them.

"Imitator, what's that?" the boys wanted to know.

"This imitator copies sounds that other birds make. It will even try to copy some sounds you make if it hears you. It is called a **lyrebird** (ˈlīrˈbûrd)."

Lyrebird

The brown earth was covered with fallen leaves. They snapped and crackled as the family continued their walk in silence. In spite of the fallen leaves, the trees were still green. As the old leaves dropped to the ground, new buds appeared to take their place.

"Mother, I almost forgot to tell you." Kathryn broke the silence. "A man was hurt at the beach yesterday. He was in the water and didn't hear the lifesaver call **'Shark** (shärk)! Shark!' until it was too late. The shark bit his leg off."

"I heard something about it at work yesterday too," Father added.

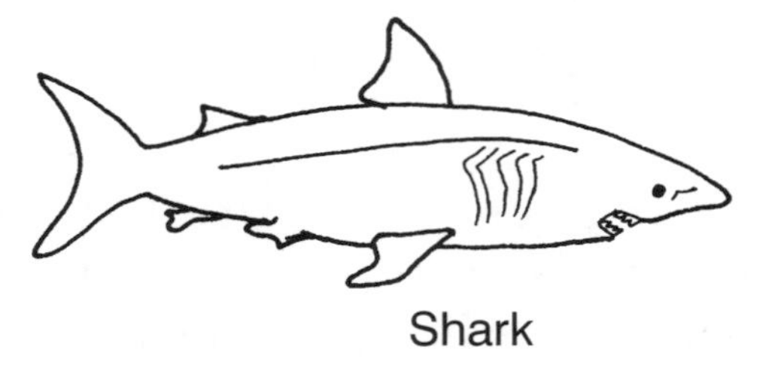
Shark

"The new girl, Heidi, from Europe told me about it," Kathryn said. "She is the girl I was telling you about last week."

"Where does she live?" Mother asked.

"They are building a new house near our Infant School (a school for grades one and two)," Kathryn replied. "It is like our house, brick with a tiled roof. She thinks that it will be much different from her home in Europe. Is there a new man working where you are, Father?"

"Not yet," Father replied. "Someone made an application at our plant last week. I'm not sure who it is or if he will get a job."

"Heidi will be able to walk partway to school with me," Kathryn declared happily.

"One of the boys in that family is in my class at school," Andrew said. "He asked me if we get lots of snow. I told him that I have never seen snow. He was surprised. He told me that snow is cold, white flakes of frozen water that float down from clouds in the sky. It covers the ground, sometimes even forming big drifts. He said they used to slide down the snow-covered hills on thin, smooth boards fastened together and having a curved-up front. He called it a toboggan."

"I have never seen snow either," Father replied. "South Australia's weather is too warm for snow. Our warm air would change cold snow to rain. We would have to go to the high mountains near the east coast of Australia to see snow."

"In Europe where your friends come from, they would not be able to have vegetables in their garden all year like we have," Father continued. "They have to get fresh carrots, broccoli, beans, and cauliflower from warmer continents. People in northern countries would not have **nectarine** (ˈnek•təˈrēn), orange, or **mandarin** (ˈman•də•rin) trees, or grapevines in their back yards as we do."

Nectarine and mandarin trees and grapevines.

"Heidi has never had **vegemite** (ˈvej•ə•mīt) sandwiches," Kathryn said. "I want to let her have one of mine sometime."

"Vegemite sandwiches are an Australian specialty." Mother smiled. "The meat pies and tomato sauce that you eat at the **canteen** (kanˈtēn—place for eating lunch) once a week are an Australian tradition too."

"Heidi likes our **pasties** (ˈpas•tēz)," Kathryn told them. "She thought they were little pies. When I told her they weren't, she cut through the crust of one and saw that it was filled with minced meat, diced potatoes, pumpkin, onion, and turnip. She really liked it."

"It's time to go home," Father announced in surprise after glancing at his watch. "We must hurry, or we will be late for supper."

CROSSWORD PUZZLE

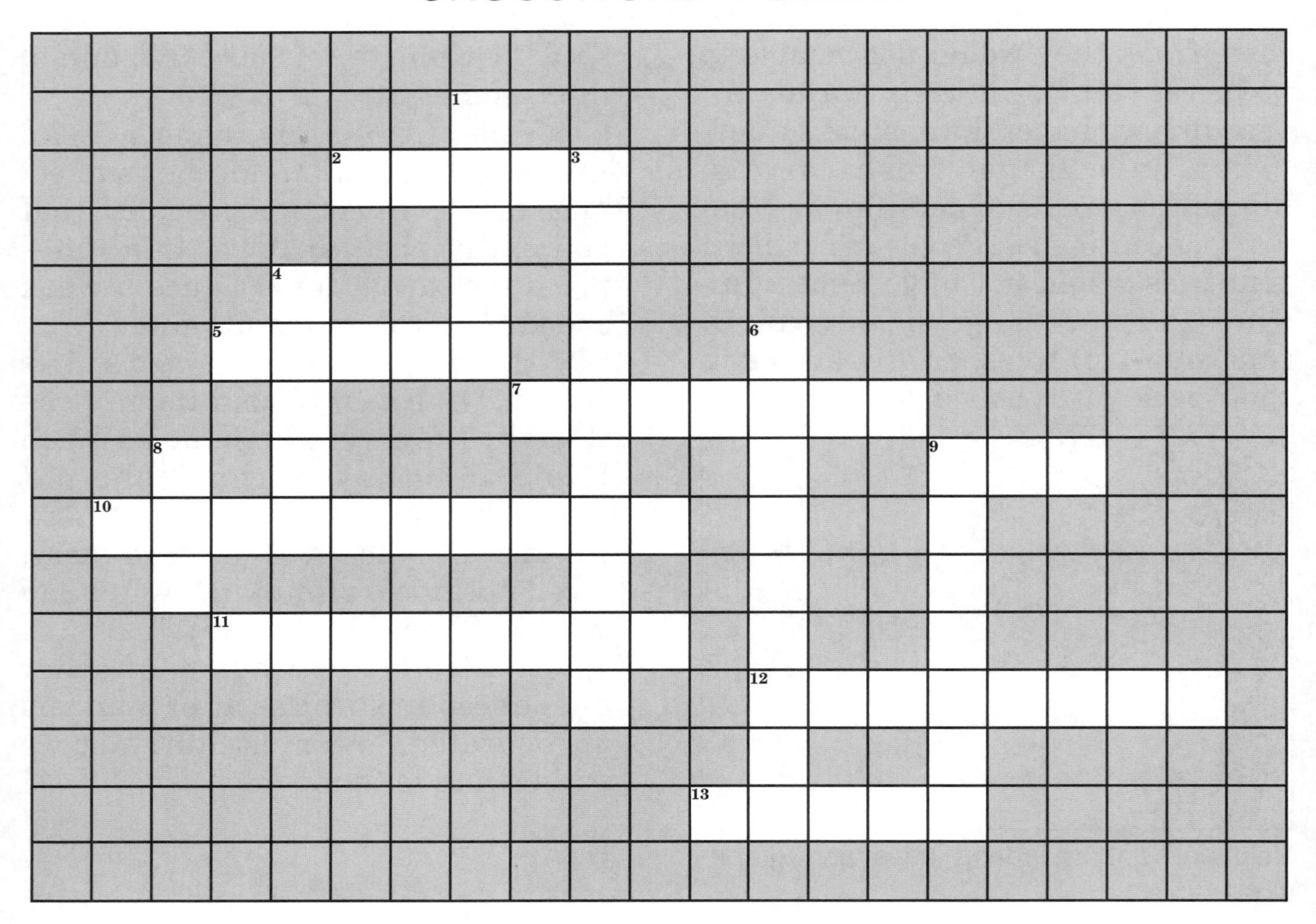

Find the word described below, and write it in the correct place on the puzzle.

Down

1. A month of the year.
3. A bird that gives a loud laughing call.
4. A little animal that looks like a bear.
6. A trained man who is to give warning if a shark is near.
8. Tall trees in South Australia.
9. Place for eating lunch at school.

Across

2. An animal that lives in the water.
5. An animal's pocket in which it carries its baby.
7. Little pies filled with meat, potatoes, and vegetables.
9. A koala's baby.
10. The kind of leaves koalas eat.
11. A bird that imitates other birds.
12. A kind of sandwich.
13. The color of Australia's earth.

22. Adoyo of Africa
Part 1

A new day was beginning to shimmer across **Lake Victoria** (Vik ˈtôr•ē•ə). Since six o'clock the sun had been casting a light across Grandmother's little kitchen on **Rusinga Island** (ro͞oˈseng•gəˈī•lənd) in Lake Victoria. Now, Grandmother was sitting on her low three-legged stool, stirring **uji** (ˈo͞o•jē) in the old earthen pot. Usually the family did not eat breakfast. But since Obonyo (ōˈbōn•yō), son of Ndege (ˈde•gē), had not eaten much supper last night, Grandmother wanted him to eat before he left for school.

"Bye-bye, Adoyo (aˈdō•yō). Bye-bye, Grandmother!" Obonyo waved toward the doorway, at the same time clutching a boiled sweet potato in his hand for his afternoon snack.

Little Adoyo waved her tiny black hand in reply. "Grandmother," she said, "I wish I were bigger so I could go to school too."

"Maybe next year," Grandmother replied. "Let's see if you are bigger now."

Adoyo reached her arm over the top of her head and tried to touch the ear on the opposite side of her head with her fingers. "I can't reach my ear

Adoyo trying to touch her ear.

yet," Adoyo sadly replied, shaking her black, curly head.

The island people did not know their ages. Since Adoyo's fingers could not touch her ear, she was not allowed to go to school. Her older brother,

Ocheche (ˈō ˈche•chē), could not go either, but that was because Father needed him to watch the cows.

"Mother, Mother," Adoyo said, running to where Mother was busily digging in the garden with her **jembe** (ˈjem•bē—a heavy hoe).

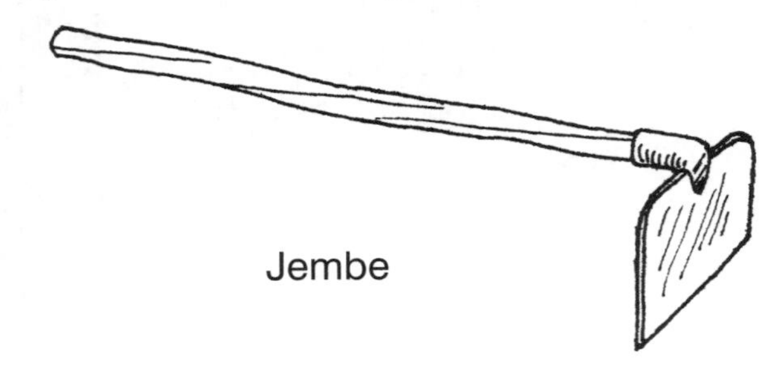

Jembe

"Good morning, little one," Mother began. "How's Mother's helper?"

"Happy," answered Adoyo joyfully, then asked, "Where are Ocheche and the cows this morning?"

"Ocheche herded them off to find grass earlier this morning," Mother explained. "The rainy March season is just beginning, you know. Yesterday they needed to go farther away from the village because the hot sun has dried up most of the grass. The boys will be taking the cows, goats, and sheep closer to the mountains. They will need to watch that the cows do not stray into the mountains, for the **hyenas** (hīˈē•nəz) will be hungry too and might kill them."

Hyena

There were many little villages on the island where Adoyo lived. In Adoyo's village there were nine people: Grandfather, Grandmother, her father Ndege, her Mother Akech (ˈak ech), Ocheche, Obonyo, Adoyo, her little brother **Okidi** (ōˈki•dē) and her baby sister Akinyi (akˈkin•yē).

Near the center of the village was the home where they all lived. The house was supported by poles standing upright. The double walls were hand **plastered** (ˈplas•tərd) with mud that had been tramped by mother's and some neighbor women's feet. The grass roof protected them from the hot sun. The well-plastered walls kept their house nice and cool.

Not too far from the main house were two little houses, Mother's kitchen and Grandmother's kitchen, where they cooked dinner and supper. Outside the village were gardens that were surrounded by hedges.

Now was a busy time for Mother and Grandmother. The gardens all needed to be dug by hand. Then the bean, corn, peanut, squash, millet, and sweet potato seeds would be planted. This morning Father was helping Mother in the garden.

"Father," Adoyo asked. "Aren't you going fishing this morning?" Father and the other men on the island spent most of their time fishing.

"I will fish this afternoon," Father replied. "If you go and ask Grandfather, he will tell you why I am helping in the garden this morning."

"The leaders of our country tell us we must start new **cassava** (kə ˈsä•və) plants every year," Grandfather explained. "So Father will plant some cassava branches in the garden when he and your mother are finished digging."

"Why must we plant them, Grandfather?" she questioned.

"Sometimes our land becomes very hot and dry after the rainy season is over. Then our plants dry up, all except for the cassava plant. Its roots go deep into the ground. If we have cassava, we can make flour for uji and **ugali** (ˈgü•lē). You watched Mother get **tapioca** (ˈtap•ēˈō•kə) from the root of this plant, didn't you?" Grandfather asked with twinkling dark eyes.

"Yes! Yes!" Adoyo exclaimed. "I like uji and ugali."

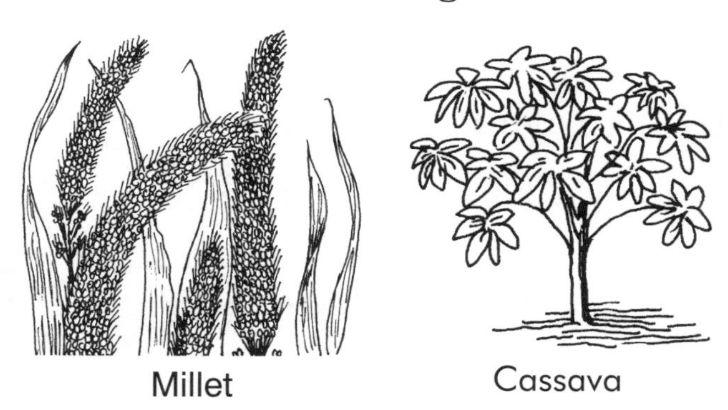

SEEING HOW WELL YOU REMEMBER

Find the part on the right that completes the sentence on the left, and write the letter on the line.

_____ 1. Adoyo was

_____ 2. Adoyo lived

_____ 3. Her brother Obonyo

_____ 4. Adoyo was too little

_____ 5. Ocheche could not go to school

_____ 6. A jembe

_____ 7. The boys who care for the cattle

_____ 8. Father and Mother dig

_____ 9. Tapioca comes from

a. because he had to watch the cows.

b. the gardens by hand.

c. on Rusinga Island.

d. must make sure the hyenas do not kill them.

e. a tiny African girl.

f. to go to school.

g. the roots of cassava plants.

h. is a heavy hoe.

i. went to school.

Read, think, and then choose the right answer from the words listed below each question.

10. Rusinga Island is an island in ______________________________.

    The Pacific Ocean　　Lake Victoria　　the Atlantic Ocean

11. The story takes place in March. Mother said that the __________ season was just beginning.

    rainy　　dry　　hot

12. The ______________________ lived in the mountains.

    families　　hyenas　　other villagers

13. The men on the island spent their time _______________________.

    in the garden　　fishing　　herding cattle

14. The villagers used a _______________ to work their gardens.

    shovel　　plough　　large hoe

15. ______________ is the only plant that does not dry up in the hot season.

    Cassava　　Sweet potato　　Ugali

16. An island is completely surrounded by ____________.

    land　　water　　gardens

23. Adoyo of Africa
Part 2

"Adoyo, Adoyo," Mother called from the corner of the house.

Adoyo quickly ran down the path. "Akinyi, Akinyi," she chanted, smiling at baby Akinyi who was tied onto Mother's back. "Are we going to the lake now?" she asked.

"Yes, we will do the washing now," Mother replied as she set a pail of clothes on top of her head and then picked up a pail in which she had placed dishes to be washed. "Okidi," she instructed, "after you have gathered wood for the fire, bring the pails down to get water." Then off they started down the path to the lake.

Grandmother also followed slowly. On her head was a **koria** (ˈkôr•ē•ə) with more dishes to wash. The koria was a flat dishpan that looked like a tray.

"Has Grandfather finished making the **canoe** (kəˈnōō) yet, Grandmother?" Adoyo asked as she walked beside Grandmother.

"No, not yet," Grandmother replied. "He is working on it now."

Soon the beautiful, blue lake was in sight. Father and men from other villages could be seen in their canoes.

"I hope they catch enough fish that they have some left to sell," Grandmother sighed, placing the koria on the ground.

"Adoyo, help Grandmother take the dishes to the water," Mother said as she untied Akinyi and set her on the ground. "Then come and watch Akinyi until we finish washing the dishes. When we are finished, you can carry her down to the water so Mother can bathe her."

Adoyo watched as Akinyi leaned

over and started to crawl toward the pile of clothes. "La, La! (No, No!)" she said as she ran to bring her back.

Akinyi crawled even faster as she saw Adoyo coming toward her. "La, La! La, La!" she copied.

Adoyo quickly caught Akinyi in her arms and gave her a stick to play with. Noticing that Mother and Grandmother were finished washing the dishes, Adoyo picked up Akinyi and carried her to Mother.

Akinyi and Adoyo had learned to love splashing in the water each day. After they finished bathing, their black hair and skin were clean and shining. The white of their eyes, and their teeth, which had had their morning rub with a soft stick, seemed to add to the gleam.

After bathing the children and themselves, Mother and Grandmother prepared to wash the clothes. In what seemed like no time, the dirty clothes had been scrubbed on the stones. Mother hung them on nearby tree branches to dry.

"There's Okidi coming," Adoyo said.

The pails swayed in Okidi's hands as he ran down the path.

"Shall I fill the pails with water?" he asked.

"Yes, bring them down to the water, and I will help you," Mother said.

Taking a smaller pail, she began to fill her own large pail. Okidi helped too and soon the pails were filled.

"First we'll carry the water pails. Then we'll get the clothes and dishes later," Mother instructed as she placed the large pail of water on her head. Grandmother tied baby Akinyi to Mother's back. Then she started up the path. Adoyo, Grandmother, and Okidi each carried a pail.

"Shall I heat water for dinner?" Grandmother asked as they set the pails of water in the little kitchen.

"Yes," Mother agreed. "After I bring the clothes and dishes up, I will start making ugali. Since there are no greens yet, maybe we can roast some of the fish Grandfather caught last evening. Okidi and Adoyo, I want you to come with me to help carry the dishes and wash home."

Adoyo's village on Rusinga Island.

By high noon they were home again. Grandmother had the water boiling and was adding some tapioca flour to make ugali. The fish were roasting over the fire.

As each member of the family got home, they sat down and began eating. The men sat at the table to eat, while the women and children sat on the floor.

After dinner, Father returned to the lake to fish. Grandfather went back to work on his canoe. Mother and Grandmother got their jembes and went to dig in the garden.

The children had a happy time playing. For a while they played in the water, but the sight of a **hippopotamus** (ˈhip•ə ˈpot•ə məs) sent them running, as fast as they could go, up the path and inside the village fence.

Hippopotamus

As usual, at three o'clock the rain started falling. Father and the other fishermen had seen the rain coming and had hurried to their villages. While the rain poured down outside, the family sat in the house and rested. By four-thirty the storm was over, and the sun was shining brightly.

The women had started making supper over an open fire in the little kitchen. When supper was ready to eat, each person took his turn holding his hands under the water that was poured from a pail. Then they sat down to a meal of ugali and fish.

After supper the little village sat and listened to Grandfather's stories until the sleepy eyes and nodding heads indicated it was bedtime. Twenty minutes after the sun set at six o'clock, Rusinga Island was in darkness.

TESTING YOUR MEMORY

Fill in the blanks.

1. Mother washed the dishes and clothes in the ______________________.
2. Okidi was given the task of gathering ______________________.
3. Mother carried Akinyi on her ______________.
4. Mother and Grandmother scrubbed the clothes on ______________.
5. Mother carried a large pail of water to the hut on her ______________.

6. Grandmother carried the dishes in a ________________.

7. For dinner and supper the family had ________________ and fish.

8. The children did not want to be in the water with the ________________.

9. Grandfather was making a ________________.

10. During the rainy season, it often starts raining around ________________ in the afternoon.

Answer the following questions in complete sentences.

11. What is a koria? ____

____

12. What two things might Father do with the fish he caught? ________________

____

13. Where did the women do their cooking? ________________________________

____

14. Where did the island people sit to eat their meals? ____________________

____

15. What did the villagers do while it was raining hard? ___________________

____

16. How did the people wash their hands? _________________________________

____

17. At what time does the sun set on Rusinga Island? ______________________

____

24. Review

Fill in the blanks. Look back at the story only if necessary.

1. A large chunk of ice floating in the water is called an ________________.
2. The type of tea that they drink in Czechoslovakia is called ________________.
3. Mr. Charvat was watched closely because he was a ________________.
4. Koalas like the leaves of the ________________ tree.
5. The mother koala carries its cub in its ________________.
6. Many schools in Australia have a ________________ where the children eat their lunch.
7. Adoyo lives on ________________ Island in Lake Victoria.
8. Her mother uses a heavy hoe called a ________________ to work the garden.
9. The people on the island plant new ________________ plants each year, because they are the only plants that do not dry up during the hot season.
10. Adoyo and her brother and sister ran from the water when they saw a ________________ nearby.

Tell in which continent you would find each of the following animals.

11. kookaburra ________________
12. wild pig ________________
13. penguin ________________
14. lyrebird ________________
15. coyote ________________
16. koala ________________
17. water buffalo ________________
18. ground hog ________________
19. parrot ________________
20. hyena ________________
21. shark ________________
22. seal ________________

People from different continents eat different foods. **Fill in the blanks beside the continents with names of foods or drinks found in the lessons. Use only foods or drinks that do not grow where you live.**

23. Australia - ________________ ________________ ________________

________________ ________________

24. Europe - ____________________

25. Africa - ________________ ________________ ________________

Match the meanings with the words by writing the correct letter on the blank.

____ 26. gum

____ 27. ice sheet

____ 28. chicory

____ 29. koria

____ 30. mandarin

a. A type of tea they drink in Europe.

b. The name of an Australian fruit.

c. A thick layer of ice and snow.

d. A type of tree that grows in Australia.

e. A flat dishpan for carrying dishes on the head.

In the rustling grass I hear Him pass—
He speaks to me everywhere.

25. Studying the Globe

"How many remember what this is?" Sister Esther asked, holding a large round object in front of her for all the grade 2 students to see.

A few hands quickly shot up. "Yes, Paul," she called.

"It is a picture of the **earth** (ûrth)," he said.

"That is right," she told him, "but does anyone remember the correct name for it? Do you remember, Brian?"

"It is a **globe** (glōb)," Brian answered.

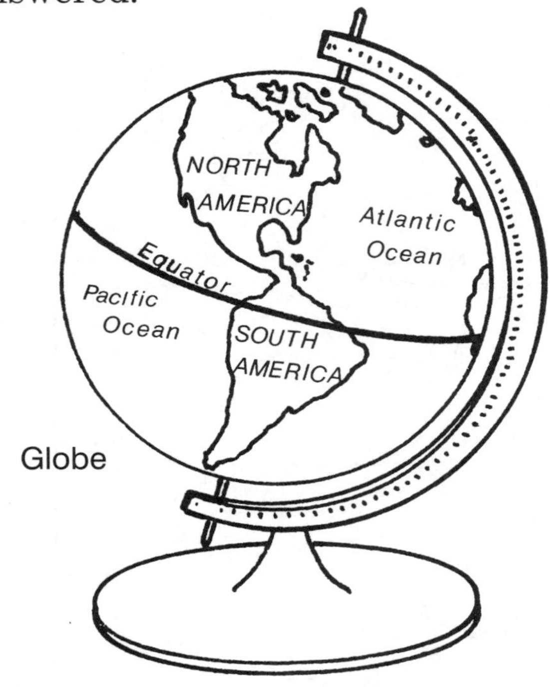

Globe

"That is correct," Sister Esther agreed.

Slowly, Sister Esther turned the globe in a circular motion on the stand, holding it so everyone could see it. Then she asked, "What color is there mostly on the map, Gary?"

"There is a lot of blue," he answered.

"Does someone remember what blue stands for on a map?" Sister Esther questioned.

"It stands for water," John replied.

"Blue also stands for water on a globe," Sister Esther explained. "Notice that much of the earth's surface is covered with water. The rest of the earth is covered with land."

"Do you remember which continent you live on?" she asked.

"North America," Joanne replied shyly.

"That's right," Sister Esther encouraged. "Now who can point to North America on the globe?"

John raised his hand, and after receiving permission, he pointed to a large green area on the top half of the globe.

Sister Esther told them more about the globe. "This is the **North Pole** (pōl)," she said, pointing to a spot at the very top of the globe. "The North Pole is the most northerly place on the earth. At the very bottom of the globe is the **South Pole.** It is the most southerly place on the earth. When we go toward the North Pole, we are going north. When we go toward the South Pole, we are going south.

"At the North Pole, there is darkness all day during the winter. When it is winter at the North Pole, it is summer at the South Pole, and the sun is seen all day long. But a half year later, the North Pole has summer, and the sun shines all day long. The South Pole then has winter with darkness all day. In most other parts of the world, the length of day changes throughout the year.

"The Bible says that as long as the earth lasts, day and night, and cold and heat will not cease," Sister Esther concluded.

DRILLING THE FACTS

On the line following the description, write the name word that is described.

1. It is round and has a picture of the earth on it. ______________________
2. It is colored blue on a globe. ______________________
3. Areas on a globe that are some color other than blue represent ______________.
4. It is a large green area on the top half of the globe ______________________.
5. It is the most northerly place on a map. ____________________
6. It is the most southerly place on a map. ____________________
7. It is seen only in summertime at the poles. ___________________

8. In most parts of the world, its length changes with the seasons. ______________________

9. During this season the sun is seen all day long at the poles. ________________

10. The poles have darkness all day long during this season. ________________

Follow these directions on the globe at the bottom of the page.

1. Color the land green.
2. Color the water blue.
3. Draw an arrow and label the North Pole.
4. Draw an arrow and label the South Pole.

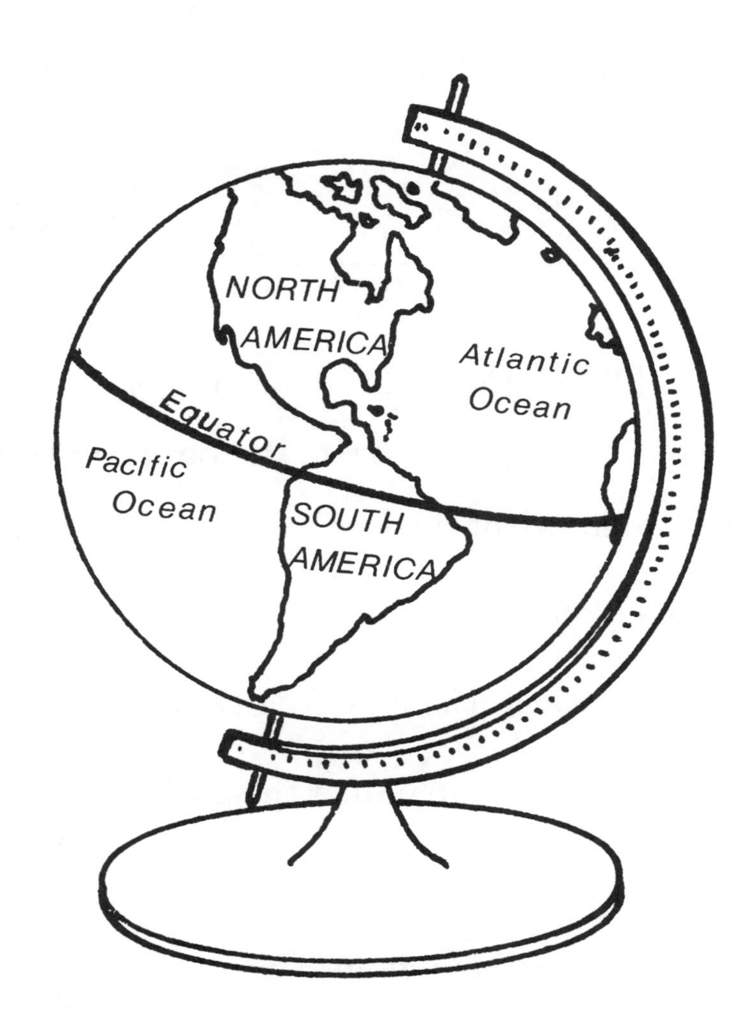

Dark northern days.

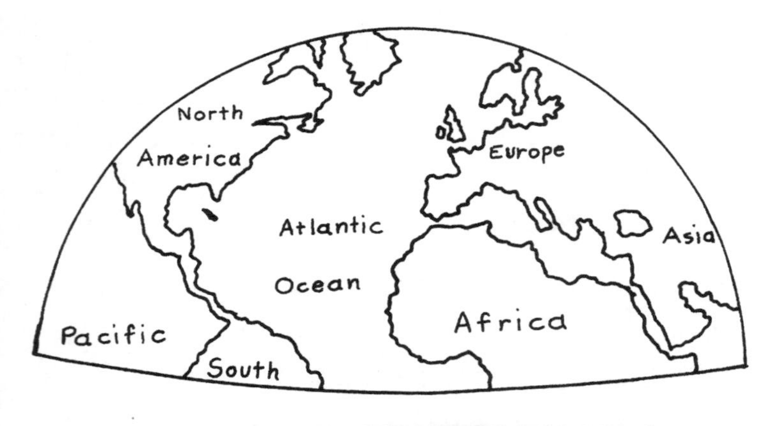

NORTHERN HEMISPHERE

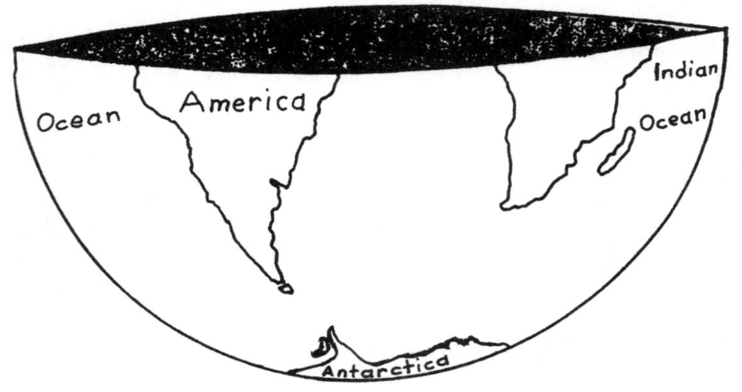

SOUTHERN HEMISPHERE

26. The Four Hemispheres

"Yesterday we learned where the north and south poles are," Sister Esther began as she lifted the globe from the desk. "Who can show me where the North Pole is?"

Eagerly the class raised their hands. "Susan, you may point to it," Sister Esther permitted.

A beaming Susan approached the globe. "Right here," she said, pointing to the top of the globe.

"That's right," Sister Esther assured her. "Now who can show us where the South Pole is?"

John was given permission this time, and walking forward, he pointed to the bottom of the globe.

"Today," Sister Esther continued, "we want to notice a line on the globe that is halfway between the North and South Poles. This line is called the equator (i`kwa ter). On the earth there is no actual line at the equator. We just think of it as being a line.

"The part of the earth above this line is the **northern** ('nor•thərn) half of the earth. The part of the earth below this line is the **southern** ('suth•ərn) half of the earth. Is Ontario in the northern or southern half of the earth?"

"In the northern half," Charles answered.

"That's right," Sister Esther replied. "All of North America is in the northern half of the earth."

"Is South America in the southern half of the earth then?" John asked.

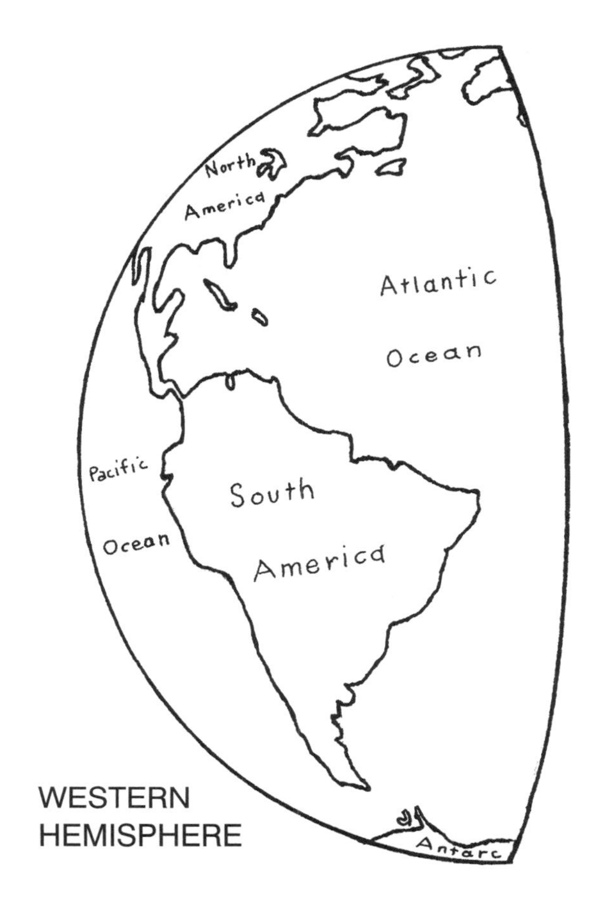

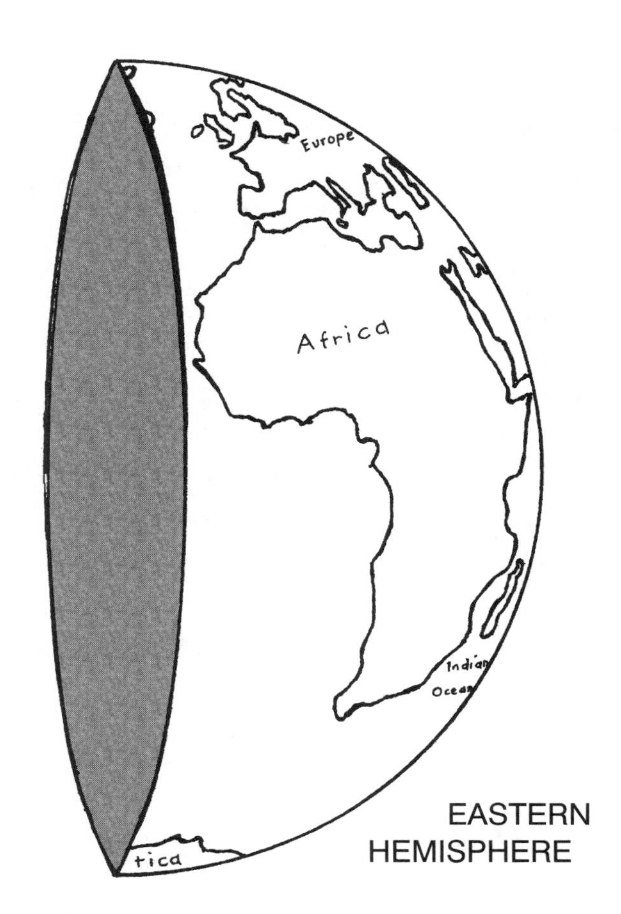

"Most of it is," Sister Esther answered, "but some of it is in the northern half. The equator passes through South America and Africa, so that part of them is in the northern half of the earth, and part of them is in the southern half.

"We can also divide the earth another way. Do you see this line on the globe that starts at the North Pole, passes through the Atlantic Ocean, and goes down to the South Pole? On the opposite side of the globe is another line that passes through the Pacific Ocean from the North Pole to the South Pole.

"The part of the earth where we live is known as the **western** (ˈwes•tərn) half of the earth. The continents on the opposite side of the earth are in the **eastern** (ˈes•tərn) half of the earth.

"Paul," she said. "Find Australia on the globe. Is it in the western or eastern half of the world?"

"Eastern," Paul answered.

"That's right," Sister Esther said. "Susan, is South America in the western or eastern part of the world?"

"Western," Susan answered thoughtfully.

"Right." Sister Esther nodded. "North and South America are the only continents completely within the western part of the world. All the other continents except Antarctica are in the eastern half of the world. Antarctica is partly in the eastern and partly in the western half of the world."

DRILLING THE DIVISIONS

Tell which part of the earth these are in.

1. Are the following in the northern or southern half of the earth?
   a. North America ______________
   b. South America ______________
   c. Australia ______________
   d. Africa ______________
   e. Europe ______________
   f. Asia ______________
   g. Antarctica ______________

2. Are the following in the eastern or western half of the earth?
   a. South America ______________
   b. Indian Ocean ______________
   c. Asia ______________
   d. Europe ______________
   e. Australia ______________
   f. North America ______________

Color the globe divisions in this lesson.

3. Color all the water blue.
4. Color the land in the northern part green, the southern part yellow, the western part pink, and the eastern part purple.

27. Learning About Rivers and Lakes

"Do you see the blue lines in each continent on this map?" Sister Esther asked the class who was gathered around the map. "Generally the lines are very winding, through some are straighter than others. Some are long and some are short. They represent **rivers** (ˈriv•ərz).

"A river is a stream of moving water. The moving of the water is called the **current** (ˈkur•ənt). You may have thrown sticks into a river and noticed that they all floated away the same direction. They were following the current.

"The **source** (sôrs) of a river is the place where it begins. The source of most rivers is a spring, a lake, or a glacier in the mountains.

"You have heard of a bed and a bank," Sister Esther went on. "A river has a bed and a bank also." Then, seeing the puzzled looks on the pupils' faces, she explained, "The bed of a river is the bottom of the course where the water flows. The bank of a river is the rising ground at the edge of the river.

"The deepest part of a river is called the **channel** (ˈchan•əl). This is usually in the middle of the river.

"The place where a river empties into a larger body of water is called its **mouth** (mouth). A river is generally widest at its mouth.

"Sometimes a river picks up sticks, sand, and other objects that lie along the river bank and carries them to the mouth of the river where they drop to the bottom. As this ground builds up higher and higher, little islands are formed.

"Many cities and towns were built beside rivers before roads were built. Then ships could sail up the river and bring their goods right to the town. The people loaded the goods that they had made and wanted to sell onto the ships. Then they were carried to other countries and continents.

"The land beside a river is often very good for growing crops. The river water can also be used to water the crops.

"A **lake** (lāk) is different from a river. A lake is a large body of inland water. Some lakes are so wide you cannot see across them. Many rivers either run into or out of lakes.

"The water in a lake is standing still. Sometimes, however, when there is a strong wind, there will be waves on the surface of the lake.

"Many cities are built beside lakes. Ships can travel on the lakes. Many people get fish from the lakes. Rivers and lakes are very useful and beautiful parts of God's creation."

A river and its parts.

NORTH AMERICA
Yukon R.
Mackenzie R.
Peace R.
Athabasca R.
CANADA
Columbia R.
Saskatchewan R.
Lake Superior
Ottawa R.
St. Lawrence R.
Missouri R.
Lake Huron
Lake Michigan
L. Erie
L. Ontario
Sacramento R.
UNITED
STATES
Arkansas R.
Ohio R.
Mississippi R.
Red R.
Rio Grande R.
Conchos R.
MEXICO
Moctazuma R.
Balsas R.

LEARNING THE NAMES OF RIVERS AND LAKES

Use the map on page 105 to find the names of these rivers.

1. The name of the river that separates Canada and the United States on the east is the ______________________________ River.

2. The ______________________________ River forms part of the border between the United States and Mexico.

3. Write the names of three rivers in Canada

   a. ______________________________ River

   b. ______________________________ River

   c. ______________________________ River

4. Write the names of three rivers in the United States.

   a. ______________________________ River

   b. ______________________________ River

   c. ______________________________ River

5. Write the names of two rivers in Mexico.

   a. ______________________________ River

   b. ______________________________ River

Four large lakes form part of the border between Canada and the United States. A fifth lake is near these lakes, but is completely in the United States. These five lakes together are called the Great Lakes.

Find the lakes on the map, and write their names below.

6. Lake ____________________
7. Lake ____________________
8. Lake ____________________
9. Lake ____________________
10. Lake ____________________

Fill in the blanks below with the correct word from the story.

11. A narrow, winding body of moving water is called a ____________________.
12. A large body of still water is called a ____________________.
13. The moving of water is called the ____________________.
14. The place where a river begins is called its ____________________.
15. The place where a river empties into a larger body of water is its ____________________.
16. The bottom of the course where the water flows is called the ____________________ of the river.
17. The rising ground at the edge of the river is the ____________________.
18. The ____________________ is the deepest part of the river.
19. Rivers and lakes are colored ____________________ on a map.
20. ____________________ travel on rivers and lakes.

28. Learning About Cities

"Today we will learn some things about cities (ˈsit•ēz)," Sister Esther began. "What do you see in the foreground of the picture at the top of page 108?"

"Ships on the water," answered Gary.

"Yes. Ships carry freight from one city to another. One city produces more of some goods than its people can use. It does not produce some other things that its people need. Ships carry the goods that a city produces but cannot use to a city where those supplies are needed. It returns with products needed by the former city.

"What goods might be shipped from a city?" Sister Esther asked the class.

"When we drove through one city last summer, we saw many grain elevators beside the water," Gary answered. "Men were loading grain onto a ship."

"We saw a ship being loaded with coal one time when we were at the city," Paul added.

"We saw men unloading timber from railroad cars and loading it onto a ship," Susan supplied.

"When we were in the North, we saw men loading paper into a ship," John said.

"You have named several goods," Sister Esther encouraged. "Ships haul many other things also. Many men are needed to load and unload the ships, and to buy and sell the goods that the ships haul.

"Men build factories in or near cities," Sister Esther continued. "Goods such as paper, steel, and furniture are made at factories. Cars, trucks, and airplanes are made and put together in factories. Hundreds of men work in a single factory. Most of these men live in a city.

"What other buildings would you see in a city?" Sister Esther asked the class.

"Stores and shops," Gary suggested.

"Schools, police stations, and hospitals," Doris offered.

"Train stations, bus stations, and airports," Paul stated.

A store in the city.

"Post offices and libraries," Susan added.

"That is right," Sister Esther commended. "And there are many others. There are buildings that contain doctors' offices, dentists' offices, and offices of businessmen. There are large bank buildings and apartment houses. People move to the city because of the many job possibilities. The presence of these people creates a need for schools, stores, libraries, post offices, bus services, airports, train stations, and so on. All of these places make more jobs for more people. And so cities continue to grow and spread out year after year."

On a map, the location of a city is represented by a black dot (•). Large cities are represented by a large dot. The location of a capital city is represented by a star (★).

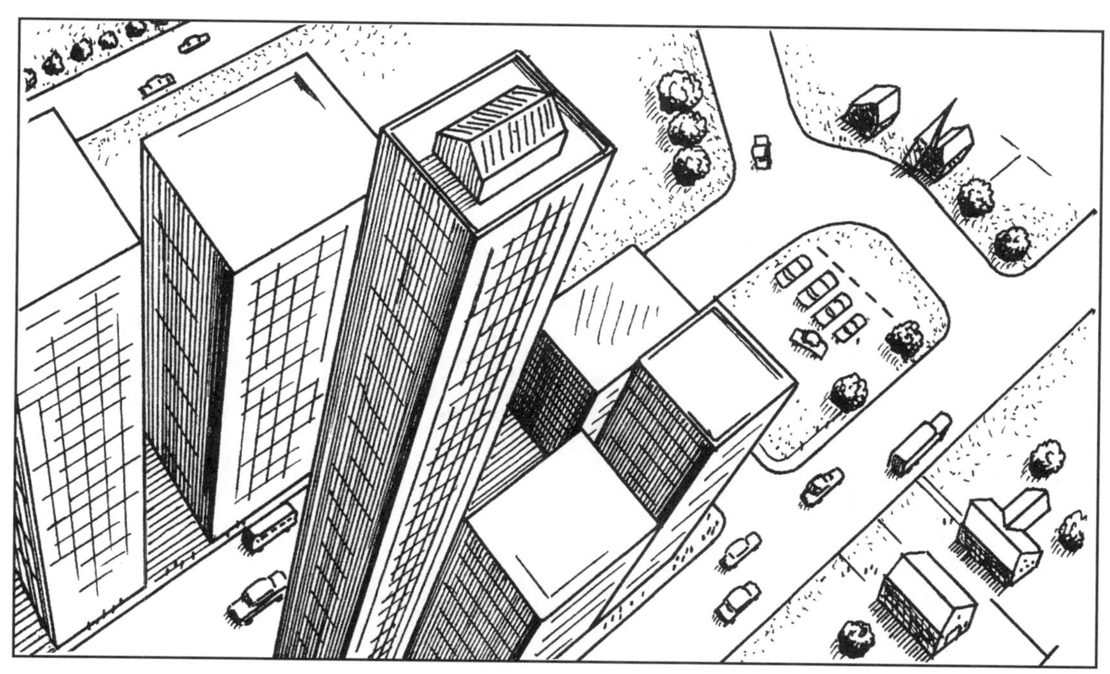
Buildings and streets in a city.

Edmonton
Calgary
Vancouver
Winnipeg
Montreal
Ottawa
Toronto
New York
Chicago
Philadelphia
Washington, D.C.
San Francisco
Los Angeles
Mexico City
NORTH AMERICA

LOCATING PLACES ON A MAP

Locate the following places on the map on page 110.

1. The capital city of the United States is Washington, D. C. Find Washington, D.C., on the map.
2. The capital city of Canada is Ottawa. Find Ottawa on the map.
3. New York is along the eastern coast of the United States. Find New York on the map.
4. Chicago is beside the southern shore of Lake Michigan. Find Chicago on the map.
5. Los Angeles is along the western coast of the United States. Find Los Angeles on the map.
6. Montreal is in the eastern part of Canada. Find Montreal on the map.
7. Vancouver is along the western coast of Canada. Find Vancouver on the map.

29. Review

Match the words with the meanings at the right.

_____	1. earth	a. Movement of water.
_____	2. water	b. A body of inland water.
_____	3. North Pole	c. A place where a large number of people live.
_____	4. South Pole	d. Its location on a map is represented by a star.
_____	5. current	e. The point on a globe that is farthest north.
_____	6. source	f. A picture of it is on a globe.
_____	7. mouth	g. It is colored blue on a globe.
_____	8. city	h. The place where a river begins.
_____	9. lake	i. The point on a globe that is farthest south.
_____	10. capital city	j. The place where a river empties into a larger body of water.

Find the answers to each of these riddles.

11. I am a line circling a globe. I run halfway between the North and South Poles. You cannot actually see me on the earth. My name is ______________________.

12. Many people live in me. I am divided into blocks. Generally there are street lights along my streets. There are many stores and apartment buildings in me. I am a ______________.

13. I am shaped like a ball. I am a picture of the earth's lands and water. I rotate on a stand. What am I? ____________________

14. Sometimes I move swiftly. Sometimes I move very slowly. Many cities are built beside me. Ships travel up and down on me. What am I?

____

Tell whether these continents are in the northern and southern part of the earth.

15. Australia ________________ 17. North America ________________

16. Europe ________________ 18. Antarctica ________________

Tell whether these continents are in the western or eastern part of the earth.

19. Asia ________________ 21. Australia ________________

20. South America ________________ 22. Africa ________________

30. Test

Think carefully as you answer these questions.

1. Write *mountain, desert, valley, hill,* or *prairie* on the lines to tell what type of land is being described.

   a. ______________________ Hot and dry.

   b. ______________________ Has steep cliffs.

   c. ______________________ It is located between two mountains.

   d. ______________________ A wide, flat area where grain crops are grown.

   e. ______________________ Many have snow-covered peaks.

   f. ______________________ People often use camels to cross it.

   g. ______________________ A high point in a rolling area.

   h. ______________________ Some have a timberline and a snow line.

   i. ______________________ It is very difficult to find water here.

   j. ______________________ Grain elevators can be seen a great way off.

2. Write the four main directions on the map on page 117.
3. Write the names of the seven continents and the four oceans in the correct places on the map. The names are listed below.

   North America
   South America
   Europe
   Asia
   Africa
   Australia
   Antarctica
   Pacific Ocean
   Atlantic Ocean
   Indian Ocean
   Arctic Ocean

4. In your own words tell how you should color a map. ______________________

   ____

5. Match the words with their meanings.

_____ a. Piles of sand heaped up by the wind.

_____ b. A short rest or sleep.

_____ c. A large knife used to cut down the jungle.

_____ d. A bird that walks with a clumsy waddle and is a good swimmer.

_____ e. A small animal with gray fur, large ears, and no tail.

_____ f. An Australian bird that has a call resembling loud laughter.

_____ g. A bird that can imitate the song of other birds.

1. siesta
2. koala
3. sand dunes
4. machete
5. kookaburra
6. penguin
7. lyrebird

6. Name the continent where each of these stories takes place.

_____________ a. Seebo lives here. He is not able to go to school. He eats rice. During the day, he helps take care of the water buffalo.

_____________ b. Kathryn lives where the kookaburras have their home. She can listen to a lyrebird imitate the kookaburra's call. She likes to take vegemite sandwiches to school with her.

_____________ c. Adoyo's home is on an island in this continent. She has black skin and shining white teeth. Her mother goes to the lake to wash the clothes. She cooks ugali on an outdoor fire. Adoyo cannot go to school because she is too small.

_____________ d. John goes to school. He learns about maps. He learns about the countries in the continent where he lives. He also learns about people in other continents.

_______________ e. Men visit this continent to study the weather and the forms of life on the continent.

_______________ f. Roberto lives near an Americano. He is not able to go to school yet. His father hoes beans. Wild pigs and parrots live on this continent.

_______________ g. Maria lives in a country where the leaders do not allow the people to read the Bible. She does not wear a red scarf because her parents are Christians. The children from non-Christian homes make fun of her.

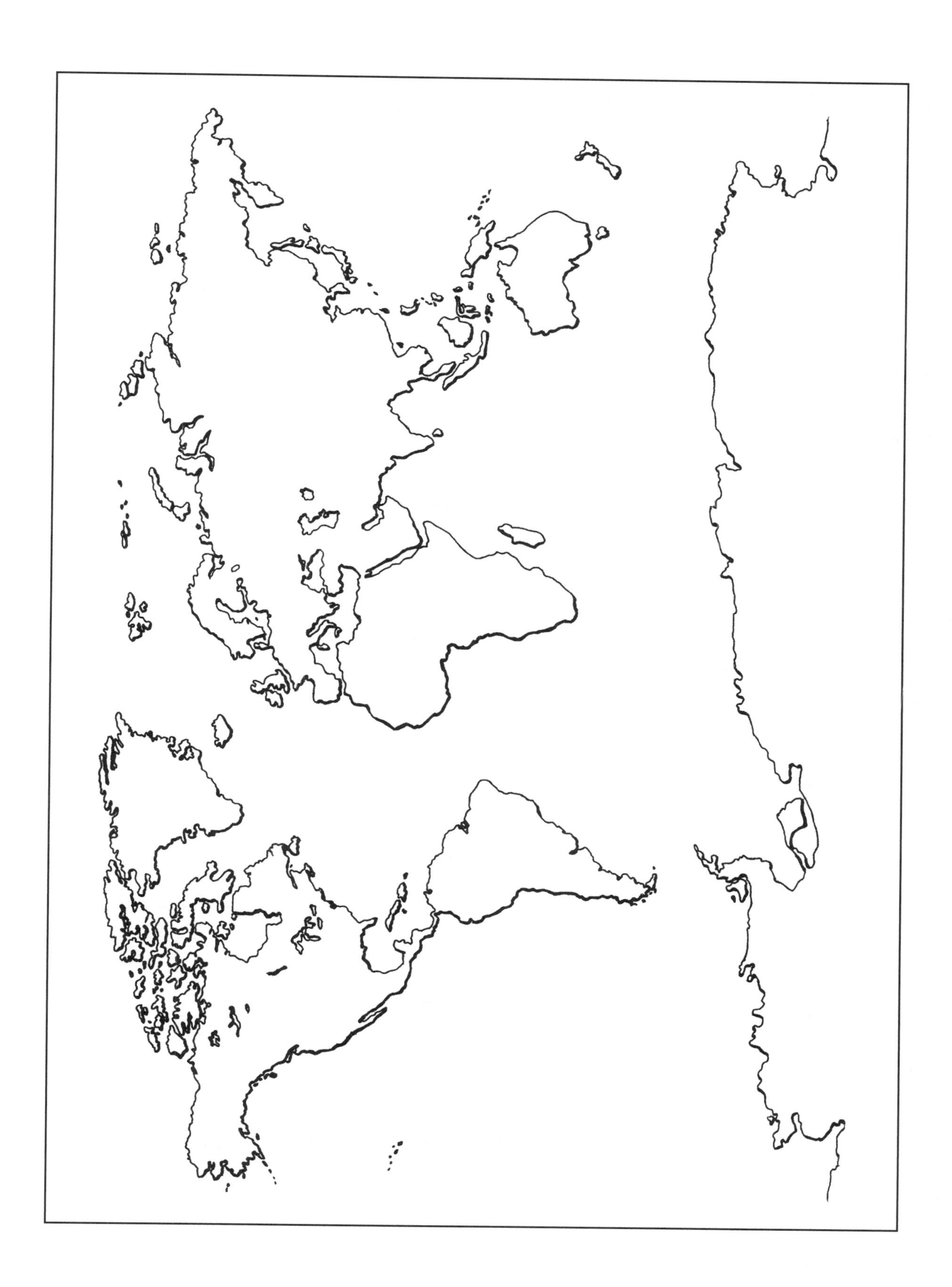

NEW WORD EXERCISES

Choose from the story the words in dark print that fit in the blank.

Lesson 1

1. ____________________ is sawn at a sawmill.

2. A store and a few houses were in the _________________.

3. The beaver _______________________ stops much of the water from flowing down the streams.

4. Some people live in a town, and some live in the ________________.

5. __________________ is the name of a province in Canada.

Lesson 2

1. ___________________ is the province next to Ontario.

2. A large area of flat, treeless land is called a ____________________.

3. A ___________________ is a doglike animal.

4. An ___________________ is a building where grain is stored.

5. ______________________ _______________________ are banks of sand piled up by the wind.

6. Manitoba is a _______________ of Canada.

7. The Byers saw sand dunes in the province of _______________.

8. _______________ is the province between Manitoba and Alberta.

Lesson 3

1. Lower hills at the bottom of the mountain are called _______________.

2. The ____________________ ____________________ are a large range of mountains in the western part of North America.

3. The mountain ____________________ was very steep.

4. Huge trees that grow in California are called ____________________.

5. California is the name of a ____________________ in the United States.

6. ____________________ is the name of a state.

7. A ____________________ ____________________ is a long row of mountains.

Lesson 4

1. The children's grandparents went for a ride up the mountain on a ____________________ ____________________.

2. The flat land along the bottom of a valley is called the ____________________ ____________________.

3. The train track wound around the side of the mountain on a narrow mountain ____________________.

4. The province of ____________________ ____________________ is in the country of Canada.

5. If a car would go over the edge of a ____________________, the passengers would probably be killed.

6. The family was glad there was a ____________________ ____________________ between the two mountains so they did not need to drive over the mountaintop.

7. A ____________________ is a frozen river of ice and snow that remains all year.

Lesson 5

1. Moses, Aaron, and Miriam lived in the land of ____________________.

2. __________________ __________________ is the name of a very dry area near Egypt.

3. Men water camels at a spring in a desert ________________.

4. Lands near the __________________ are often very hot.

5. A ____________________ is dry, sandy land.

6. A _____________ can walk a long time in the desert without drinking water.

Lesson 7

1. Ontario is a province in the country of ___________________.

2. The third largest country in North America is ____________________.

3. A ___________________ is a large mass of land.

4. We can find a picture of the countries of the world in a book called an ________________.

5. Canada and the United States and Mexico are countries in the continent of _____________________ ___________________.

6. _________________ __________________ is the continent below Central America.

7. ____________________ ____________________ is the country between Canada and Mexico.

Lesson 8

1. The fifth largest continent is ______________________.

2. ______________________ is an island continent.

3. The longest river in the world is found on the continent of ______________________.

4. ______________________ is the largest continent. It has the little word as in it.

5. The word rope is in the word ______________________. It is the sixth largest continent.

Lesson 10

1. A very large body of water is called an ______________________.

Lesson 13

1. A region that grows a large amount of grain is often called a ______________________.

2. Iron is the name of a ______________________ that is found beneath the earth's surface.

3. Wood is ground into a soft, juicy material called ______________________ from which paper is made.

4. ______________________ are holes dug in the earth from which coal, minerals, or precious stones are taken.

Lesson 14

1. A ____________________ is a short sleep or rest.

2. ____________________ are tall plants with bright yellow flowers.

3. The bean of the ____________________ plant is a source of oil and flour.

4. José was hunting a ____________________ so his mother could make soup.

5. ____________________ is the Spanish word for soup.

6. ____________________ is the Spanish word for American.

7. ____________________ is the language many of the people in Paraguay speak. Roberto would learn that language if he went to school.

8. ____________________ are dark, reddish beans similar to kidney beans.

9. A ____________________ is a cone-shaped fruit tipped with spiked leaves.

10. A ____________________ is a hat with a wide brim.

11. David placed a stone in a ____________________ and hurled it at the giant Goliath. José intended to kill a parrot with one.

Lesson 15

1. ____________________ are long yellowish fruit that grow in clusters on a plant. Carlos was taking a load of them to town on his cart.

2. A ____________________ is a heavy knife. Roberto's father used it to chop down the jungle.

3. A ____________________ is a thick growth of high grass, vines, brush, or trees.

4. A ____________________ is a large farm where horses, cattle, or sheep are grazed.

5. A ______________ ______________ is a pig that is running wild in the jungle.

6. ______________ herd and take care of cattle on a ranch.

7. The people placed the branches of a ______________ ______________ before Jesus when He rode into Jerusalem. This kind grow in the jungle where Roberto's father was working.

Lesson 16

1. Seebo is tribal ______________ boy. He is called an Indian because he lives in India.

2. A ______________ is a cotton, towel-like shoulder piece.

3. A ______________ ______________ is an animal with a large set of horns that enjoys being in the water.

4. Seebo is a ______________ Indian boy. This means that his way of life is similar to that of the people around him, but different from that of people in other areas.

5. ______________ is the name for the type of lunch pail Seebo used.

Lesson 17

1. The boys found ______________ ______________ in the field.

2. The people in India put ______________ on their rice.

Lesson 19

1. ______________ are large chunks of ice floating in the ocean.

2. A covering of ice and snow that covers Antarctica all year long is called an ______________ ______________.

3. A ____________________ is a bird that walks with a clumsy waddle and likes to swim in the water.

Lesson 20

1. The ____________________ had told Father Charvat where he must work when he got out of school.

2. ____ is the name of a country in Europe.

3. People drink ____________________ tea.

4. The Czechoslovakian name for this tea is ____________________.

5. Another name for policemen is ____________________.

6. Pictures of the leader of ____________________ were on the walls of the school.

Lesson 21

1. A ____________________ is a large, dull gray fish that is sometimes dangerous to man. One bit a man's leg off when he was in the water.

2. A ____________________ is a pocket where an animal carries its young. The koala sometimes carried its cub in this pocket.

3. Australian children eat their lunch in a ____________________.

4. ____________________ is a large evergreen tree that is useful for its gum, oil, and wood. The koala that Kathryn saw was in one of these trees.

5. A ____________________ is a small animal with gray fur, large ears, and no tail. Its favorite meal is eucalyptus leaves.

6. A lyrebird is an ____________________ since it copies sounds made by other birds.

7. ________________ is a type of sandwich eaten in Australia.

8. A ______________________ is an Australian bird, which has a call resembling loud laughter.

9. A ______________________ copies sounds made by other birds or even by people.

Lesson 22

1. ______________________ ______________________ is the name of a large body of water in Africa.

2. Adoyo's mother uses a ______________________ to work the garden.

3. Tapioca is obtained from the roots of the ______________________ plant.

4. ______________________ is the dried starch from the root of the cassava plant.

5. ______________________ ______________________ is the name of an island in Lake Victoria.

6. ______________________ are wolflike animals with short hind legs and strong teeth. Ocheche guarded the cows so they would not be eaten by these animals.

7. ______________________ and ______________________ are made from the flour of the cassava plant.

8. ______________________ walls have a coating of water and mud or some other material on them.

Lesson 23

1. A ______________________ is a long, narrow boat pointed at both ends. Grandfather was making one.

2. A ______________________ is a flat dishpan that looks like a tray.

3. A ______________________ has short legs and a large, hairless body and can swim in the water. The children ran to get inside the village fence when they saw one.

Lesson 25

1. A globe has a picture of the ______________ on it.
2. The ______________ has a picture of the earth on it.
3. The most southerly point on a globe is the ______________ ______________.
4. The most northerly point on a globe is the ______________ ______________.

Lesson 26

1. The bottom half of a globe is the ______________ half.
2. The top half of a globe is the ______________ half.
3. North and South America are in the ______________ part of the globe.
4. The other continents are in the ______________ part of the globe (except for Antarctica which is in both).

Lesson 27

1. The ______________ is the place where a river empties into a larger body of water.
2. The deepest part of a river is called the ______________.
3. A body of inland water is called a ______________.
4. A ______________ is a stream of water.
5. The moving of a river is called the ______________.
6. The place where a river begins is its ______________.

Lesson 28

1. ______________________ are places where large numbers of people live.

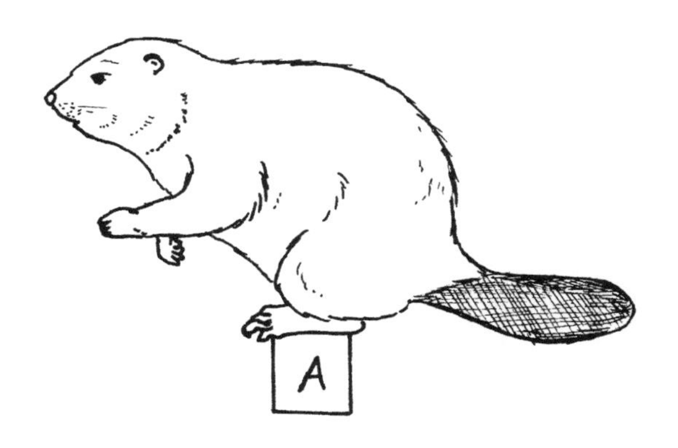

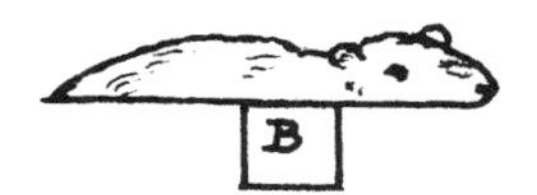

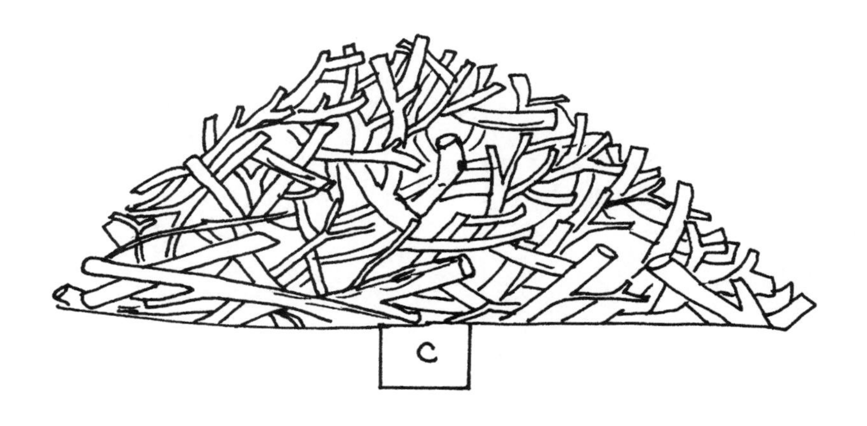

Cutouts for Lesson 1, page 12.

Cutouts for Lesson 7, page 35.

Cutouts for Lesson 7, page 36.